SHINE: Hidden No Longer

Sisters Light Up the World
Through Speaking Truth to Power

by Andrea L. Dudley

For Mercedes,
You are a
beautiful
flower & blessed
and more
blessed

Printed in the United States of America
ISBN 978-1974088591

 Editors: Linda Weatherly and Caroline D. Parker.

Cover Design: Habakkuk Publishing
Printed in the U.S.A.

Table of Contents

Dedication v

Foreword
Dr. Alta Davis..1

SHINE
Ameerah Lewis..5

I Will Shine Again!
Andrea Dudley 7

The Occulere: Removing the Shroud of Darkness
Dr. Anya Miller Hall...21

Shine Special Feature: You Are Empowered to Do Exploits
Rev. Dr. Margaret E. Benson Idahosa Archbishop and
Trailblazer 27

Inspirational Affirmations
Dr. Margaret E. Benson Idahosa 35

You Are Brilliant: All You Need Is a Good Polish
Sima L. Ballinger, B.B.A..41

Dream Awake... and Become the Miracle of Your Brilliance
Pastor Judith Cooper...49

Hidden Frustrations
Pastor Regina Burrell...57

All the Naysayers, Have a Seat to the Left!
Rev. Arnita M. Traylor 63

Traveling Grace
Rev. Helene M. Walker..73

When Life Creates the Perfect Storm
Rev. Joyce Irvin Harris, M.Div..81

Can I Not Do with You?
Rev. Doris B. Ryans 91

Teach Me to Shine
Linda Thornton M.A. NCC/LPC, ACS 99

Shine Special Feature: I'm a Survivor
Dr. Eunice Mosley Dudley Humanitarian and Entrepreneur 107

Shining Past the Veil of Rejection
Tanya R. Bankston, MA, CLC, SST 117

The One Thing
Anita Newby 125

Finding My Voice
Tiara Curry 135

Water Your Own Garden
Zabrina Gordon...143

Shining in the Light: A Designer's Original
Pastor Darlene Thorne, M.Div. 151

From Shame to Shine: A Journey
Caroline D. Parker 159

Outside the Gate
Minister LaVondia Eldridge 169

Shine Special Feature: Understanding the New Rules of Money
Jewel Tankard International Business and Media Mogul with
Andrea L. Dudley Visionary Publisher...179

Shine Like a Diamond? Can I Get out from Under the Dirt First?
Evangelist Valerie Parker Robinson...187

Conclusion
Andrea L. Dudley 197

Acknowledgments...205

About Andrea L. Dudley
Visionary Publisher, Speaker, and Transformation Coach.............207

DEDICATION

This book is dedicated to those who recognize the need for change in their lives and are willing to put in the work to make it happen. Our hope is that, as a result of reading this book, you will take courage and change your life for the better. That you will shine in dark places and allow the light of Jesus Christ to bring illumination to others through you.

This book is also dedicated to all the women of the world who fight to let their light shine in the lives of the people around them. Women truly do light up the world.

It is also dedicated to the tribe of people who love and support me on a daily basis in real life, through Facebook and other social media outlets. I love and appreciate each of you.

To my loving and amazing husband, Michael, and my three gifted children: Solomon, Princeton, and Andrea Amere: I am so excited about the big dreams that you have. Never allow anyone to steal your dreams. To my granddaughter, Ashlyn Hope: I've learned so much from you...all about life and love and what matters most.

Harness the power of dreams by giving yourself permission to dream with God and tap into who He created you to be. Thank you for giving me the gift of having you in my life!

Foreword

Dr. Alta Davis

I am privileged to have known and collaborated with Andrea Dudley, the visionary publisher and creator of the inspirational "Talitha Cumi" series of powerful books. These books have changed the lives of hundreds of women and this new entry: *Shine: Hidden No Longer: Sisters Light Up the World Through Speaking Truth to Power* (hereafter *Shine*) is the best in the series.

From the beginning of time, women have endured horrendous experiences that threatened the very lifeline of their existence. Women have long been exposed to an environment that advocates limitations. Yet, they are still expected to be "strong" and have the ability to multi-task only in the role society approves. The nurturing qualities and characteristics of women have been warped by social conditioning that denies the recognition of their creative spirit. The ideation of and limitations on women has reinforced the "weaker vessel as support only syndrome" that society has dictated for decades. This syndrome perhaps fuels the well-known but fatally flawed notion of the "Superwoman." Women have greatly suffered in the darkness of self-destruction by trying to live up to this irrational expectation.

In *Shine*, Andrea has chosen a talented group of authors with diverse and powerful stories who authentically capture how they overcame the darkness of difficult life situations. Andrea's work with this anthology and the authors' transparency will surpass the reader's expectation. *Shine* is an impeccable masterpiece that amplifies the reward of overcoming pain, trauma, abuse, shame, intimidation, and more of life's challenges. This book takes the reader beyond mere narrative to a primer on how to break free of the bondages of the mind, body, and spirit. The authors in *Shine* capably demonstrate their ability to "speak truth to power" by refusing to live a powerless and ineffective life.

The powers of darkness that sometimes overtake women can originate from several causes: an extensive period of illness, a suppressed ability to function normally, a lack of healthy self-esteem, or a simple fear of failure. Fear of failure can so paralyze women that not wanting to face it can become comfortable like a crutch. For the wounded or the maimed, a crutch is something that engenders more and more dependence on walking awry. After a time, the use of the crutch can mold itself into the psyche of the person who is crippled. Use of emotional crutches can cause a woman to become accustomed to living in abnormality. However, a transformative power is unleashed when a woman refuses to stay in a place of darkness. Healing begins when a woman is determined to cast aside that which cripples her. Only then can she stand in the power of Godly strength.

Shine exposes the bondages of depletion and dark despair that occur when a woman's voice and power are shut down. Through their stories, the authors speak to women who feel they have insufficient faith because of the agonizing pain that enshrouds them in darkness. These stories of women who have successfully cast off the darkness and moved into the light are empowering. Reading about the authors' transformations in *Shine* is akin to a person who climbs out of a dark cave into the bright revelation of wholeness.

I am reminded of a story in the Bible about a Queen named Esther. Esther began her life at a disadvantage. She lost her parents at an early age and was raised by a much older male cousin named Mordecai. She was kidnapped in order to fulfill an edict of the king and taken from all she knew. If we look at the bare bones of her life, we could say that it was touched by darkness. She had no parents. She didn't have the freedom to live her life as she chose. When taken to the king's court, she had to lie about her name and her heritage. Though she was eventually made Queen of Persia, an act of hatred threatened to destroy her. She was doomed to death because one man wanted to annihilate her people. But Esther faced the darkness with courage. She went unbidden to the king's court to beg his favor. In those days, if the king didn't summon you and you came to the palace uninvited, you were executed. But when Queen Esther showed up with the Light of God and justice surrounding her, King Xerxes granted her an audience. Emboldened by the power of God, Esther triumphed over the darkness that tried to crush her very existence. Because she faced darkness and fear by faith in her God, Queen Esther made her case before the king, and she and her people were saved.

The pointed, anointed pen of these writers rips open psychological strongholds that attempt to keep women in darkness through the fortress of the abnormal and/or the unhealthy. The lingering effects of deviance brought on by emotional, mental, sexual, and physical abuse have plagued women for far too long. Adversity often brings fear and self-doubt along as "company" to help stifle any progress of moving forward. Consistently being attacked by inner and societal norms seriously encumbers women on a consistent basis. In fact, we women often heartlessly judge one another by making unfair and caustic assumptions about another woman's character. We do so even though we have neither knowledge nor understanding of the depth of the effects of adversity in that woman's life. The authors have tapped into how to live freely, with a refreshed and renovated mindset in the light of God's power.

The authors in *Shine* have overcome devastating obstacles that tried to shut out the unique qualities of gifts and talents that make them who they are. Some of these authors have had to go back to the womb of painful rejection that impeded the growth that God created them for. Some have had to go back to visit past atrocities of dire and uncomfortable circumstances to free themselves and the reader as well. Some have been fighting since childhood to regain momentum and overcome shame in order to live a life of joy and peace. They reach out willing hands and hearts to assist with the healing of those who are yet coming forth. *Shine* is a catalyst for changing one's mindset from "No, I can't!" to "Yes, I can!"

As you read these writings, I encourage you to reflect on how defeating negative circumstances brought hope and healing to these authors. I believe that this is the season of renewal, especially your renewal. It is a time for you to move forward with great courage, faith, and trust.

I am grateful to have been a participant of this great work and I applaud the women who honestly and openly bared their souls in this excellent and powerful labor of love.

Dr. Alta Davis
Senior Pastor, Compassion Ministries Outreach
Director of Abundant Restoration Inc. Counseling, LPC

SHINE

Prophetic Poetry

Ameerah Lewis

Rise up Daughters of Zion,
and take your rightful place.
Rise UP you Daughters of the Most High God!
And take your rightful places.
You mothers, you daughters, you preachers, you teachers, you prophets, you evangelists, and apostles: Get in line and receive your inheritance.

Stop lurking in the shadows and come out into My marvelous light.
Let the world see your beauty.
That beauty that I hid within you before you were even born.

Shine for Me, O My Jewels.
Sparkle as you step forward into My marvelous light.
Let them SEE you!
No longer will you hide yourself in fear
and in shame.
Fear that they will see you,
the real you
as not enough...or just too much.
That you would be rejected, mocked, judged.
Let My Perfect Love cast those fears
far from you.

You are My Jewel, hide NOT your beauty from the world,
But shine for Me!
The world needs what I have hidden within you,
so let it be hidden no more!

Rise up! Oh Daughters of Zion!
Wait no longer for your destiny to begin.
Seek Me today! Receive your inheritance.
You psalmists and musicians,
you doctors and businesswomen,
you missionaries and pastors; You carriers of My Glory.

Come into the light!
Let Me watch as you sparkle for Me.
Step up! Step out! Step into your destiny.

No longer will you hide behind your work, your husbands, your children.
Allow the distractions of this world
To evaporate into mere vapor
Here in My presence.
So I can strengthen you.
So I can empower you
For our journey together.
Be set free into your destiny.

Rise and Shine!
Not just for you,
But for future generations!
For your daughters, and granddaughters...and great granddaughters.
Don't let this world steal your sparkle,
My precious, precious jewels,
For you are beautiful to Me.
And this world needs your beauty...

I WILL SHINE AGAIN!

Andrea Dudley

"There is no easy walk to freedom anywhere, and many of us will have to pass through the valley of the shadow of death again and again before we reach the mountaintop of our desires."

--Nelson Mandela

"Listen carefully: Unless a grain of wheat is buried in the ground, dead to the world, it is never any more than a grain of wheat. But if it is buried, it sprouts and reproduces itself many times over. In the same way, anyone who holds on to life just as it is destroys that life. But if you let it go, reckless in your love, you'll have it forever, real and eternal."

--The Gospel of John 12:24-25

Chippie the parakeet never saw it coming. One second he was peacefully perched in his cage. The next he was sucked in, washed up, and blown over. The problems began when Chippie's owner decided to clean Chippie's cage with a vacuum cleaner. She removed the attachment from the end of the hose and stuck it in the cage. The phone rang, and she turned to pick it up. She had barely said "hello" when Chippie got sucked in. The bird owner gasped, threw down the phone, turned off the vacuum, and opened the bag. There was Chippie...still alive, but stunned.

Since the bird was covered with dust and soot, she grabbed him and raced to the bathroom. She turned on the faucet and held Chippie under the running water. Then, realizing that Chippie was soaked and shivering, she did what any compassionate bird owner would do, she reached for the hair dryer and blasted the pet with hot air.

Poor Chippie never knew what hit him. A few days after the trauma, the reporter who had initially written about the event contacted Chippie's owner to see how the bird was recovering.

"Well," she replied, "Chippie does not sing much anymore; he just sits and stares."

It is not hard to see why. Sucked in, washed up, and blown over. That is enough to steal the song from the stoutest heart.

Chippie's story is my story and yours. Many of us have been battered, scarred, and left for dead through divorce or sickness, job loss or the death of a loved one. Each one of us has a story. It is one thing when you do not have control over things that happened to you as a child, or if you're an elderly person or someone incapable of fending for yourself. It is another thing when you allow life to happen to you and you don't take responsibility for your own actions. If you've been sucked in, washed up, and blown over, don't be like Chippie. Rise again and start singing. Shine!

The truth is, everyone will have challenges and setbacks, and we are exactly where we are supposed to be based on the decisions that we have made. We all experience life-altering obstacles that threaten to dull our shine or even extinguish our light altogether.

"Into each life some rain must fall, but too much is fallin' in mine," are the lyrics to a song.

Have you ever wondered why bad things happen to good people? Or why good people seem to endure such a rain of tremendous hardships? The truth of the matter is, we are not exempt from experiencing challenging seasons in our lives. No one will go through their life with everything coming up roses. There are times in life where everything *is* really just excellent, life *is* prosperous, and everything you touch turns to gold! The premise of this book is that you can shine even in the midst of tremendous obstacles! That when you speak "your" truth to opposing forces, your light will brightly shine. You have the power to create the life of your dreams by managing your thoughts, actions, and deeds. You can live the good life if you are willing to put in the time and discipline needed to do so. However, no one is exempt from challenges and setbacks.

The greatest achievers say that, in a lifetime of setbacks and comebacks, the truest sense of accomplishment is not found in the realization of the goal, but rather in the will to continue when failure breeds doubt.[1] Here are some examples of people who bounced back after a setback in their lives. One thing they all had in common: they never gave up!

Napoleon Hill was an American author in the area of the new thought movement. He was one of the earliest producers of the modern genre of personal success literature. He is widely considered to be one of the great writers on the subject of success. His most famous work, *Think and Grow Rich* (1937), is one of the best-selling books of all time. During his early life, Napoleon endured great disappointment, failure, and setback after setback. He overcame being broke,

---

[1] See more at: http://www.success.com/article/rich-man-poor-man#sthash.Z1YTYd6I.dpuf

divorced, destitute, and fleeing for his life before he became successful.

Dr. George Washington Carver was an African-American scientist, botanist, educator, and inventor. Dr. Carver's reputation is based on his research into and promotion of alternative crops to cotton, such as peanuts, soybeans, and sweet potatoes, which also aided nutrition for farm families. Carver was born into slavery in Diamond Grove, Missouri, and was kidnapped immediately after birth. However, he had an insatiable desire to learn, and walked ten miles every day just to attend school. He relocated many times during his youth. Carver applied to several colleges before being accepted at Highland College in Highland, Kansas. When he arrived, however, he was rejected because of his race.

Esther, a Jewish orphan girl, was raised by her cousin, Mordecai. Esther became queen of Persia and thwarted a plan to commit genocide against her people.

Bill Gates' first business failed. Yes, one of the richest persons in the whole world could not make any money at first. Traf-O-Data (a device which could read traffic tapes and process the data) failed miserably. When Gates and his business partner Paul Allen tried to sell it, the product would not even work.

Albert Einstein did not speak until he was four years old and did not have the best childhood. In fact, many people thought he was just a dud. Throughout elementary school, many of his teachers thought he was lazy and would not make anything of himself. He always received good marks, but his head was in the clouds, conjuring up abstract questions people could not understand. However, through his quirky way of thinking, he eventually developed the theory of relativity, which many of us still cannot wrap our heads around today!

Oprah Winfrey is one of the richest, most successful people in the world today, but she did not always have it so easy. She grew up in Milwaukee, Wisconsin, and was repeatedly molested by her cousin, an uncle, and a family friend. She eventually ran away from home and, at the age of fourteen, bore a baby boy who died shortly after his birth. Winfrey's tragic past did not stop her from becoming the force she is today. She excelled as an honor student in high school, and won an oratory contest which secured her a full scholarship to college. Now the entrepreneur and personality has the admiration of millions and a net worth of $2.9 billion.

Vincent Van Gogh is considered to be one of the greatest artists of all time, yet the poor guy only sold one painting the entire time he was alive: "The Red Vineyard at Arles (The Vigne Rouge)," which is now in the Pushkin Museum of Fine Arts in Moscow. Even though he made no money, he still painted over 900 works of art. Though his persistence went unnoticed when he was alive, Van Gogh proves you do not need external validation to be proud of the work you create.

Bethany Hamilton started surfing when she was just a child. At age thirteen, an almost deadly shark attack resulted in her losing her left arm. She was back on her surfboard one month later; and two years after that, she won first place in the Explorer Women's Division of the NSSA National Championships. Talk about determination!

Why Setbacks?

The online Urban Dictionary defines setback as "an interruption that keeps you from achieving something and can cause great inconvenience to your life." A setback may just knock you off your time schedule or can stop you from doing what you drastically need to do. Setbacks are not good.

The Free Dictionary defines setback as "an unanticipated or sudden check in progress; a change from better to worse; an unfortunate happening that hinders or impedes; something that is thwarting or frustrating."

Anything that takes you off your course and purpose is a setback. A setback is a hindrance or problem that interrupts your progress. It is usually temporary, like an unanticipated or sudden check in progress, or a change from better to worse. The loss of a loved one, a divorce, sickness, cancer, moving, a job change, bankruptcy, foreclosure, and becoming a caregiver are events that have the potential to cause a setback or are setbacks themselves. There has never been one person who has walked the earth who has not encountered at least one setback in their lifetime.

We live in the "real" world. We are not a part of the movie "The Truman Show" where we live in the cheerful community of Seahaven. The movie's fictional "island paradise" has weather that is always mild and no unpleasantness ever intrudes. In real life, we are constantly bombarded with news and situations that often keep us in the mode of a setback.

There are different reasons that we go through heartache, hardship, setbacks, and challenges. The most obvious reason is that all these things are a part of life. Another reason is that life is comprised of various experiences. Some are good, some are bad; some are happy and some are sad. We lose loved ones, we get divorced, we get sick, we get fired, and we lose possessions.

Pruning During Times of Setbacks

Pruning is a horticultural process involving the selective removal of parts of a plant such as branches, buds, or roots. Reasons to prune plants include deadwood removal, shaping (by controlling or directing growth), improving or maintaining plant health, reducing the risk of falling branches, preparing nursery specimens for transplanting, and both harvesting and increasing the yield or quality of flowers and fruits. The practice entails targeted removal of diseased, damaged, dead, non-productive, structurally unsound, or otherwise unwanted tissue from crops and landscape plants.

At first glance, pruning may seem to be a counter-intuitive activity because what you are pruning would seem to most to be a very healthy vine. However, it is not just the removal of what is dead. Pruning can also mean cutting away the good and the better so that we might enjoy the best.

The television show "Hoarders Alive" documents the real-life struggles and treatment of people who suffer from compulsive hoarding. Compulsive hoarding (more accurately described as "hoarding disorder") is a pattern of behavior that is characterized by the excessive acquisition of and inability or unwillingness to discard large quantities of objects that engulf the living areas of a home and causes significant distress or impairment. The reason I bring up hoarding is that, while we can be hoarders of physical things that overrun our homes and prevent us from moving around, we can also be guilty of brain hoarding: holding on to destructive, toxic thoughts and imaginations. When we are "brain hoarders," we can unfortunately hoard negative thoughts that make it very hard to get anything positive into our brains.

I once heard an interesting sermon by W. Max Alderman on the parable of the fig tree entitled: "Will God Have To Dig And Dung You?" Pastor Alderman took his text from Luke 13: 6-9.[2]

> *He spake also this parable; A certain man had a fig tree planted in his vineyard; and he came and sought fruit thereon, and found none. Then said he unto the dresser of his vineyard, Behold, these three years I come seeking fruit on this fig tree, and find none: cut it down; why cumbereth it the ground? And he answering said unto him, Lord, let it alone this year also, till I shall dig about it, and dung it: And if it bear fruit, well: and if not, then after that thou shalt cut it down. (KJV)*

Do you need a good "digging and dunging"? Sometimes, as a result of dealing with the cares of life, we become bitter, resentful, and unfruitful. Our hearts become hard and fallow, and we become barren. The master Vine Dresser believes that we are salvageable and He offers to turn over the hard places in our lives and nourish us by a process called "digging and dunging." If you have been planted in the vineyard of God, know that it is a very special place and that you have been given special treatment. You are favored. Allow the Holy Spirit to work on you. Give up the malice! Forgive those who hurt you. Stop being angry. Stop speaking negatively. "Get over it" and move on. Read the Word of God, pray, and get that much needed nourishment today.

Overcoming Major Setbacks

Breakdowns can create breakthroughs. Things fall apart so things can fall together. Having come through many setbacks

---

[2] http://www.sermoncentral.com/sermons/wll-god-have-to-dig-and-dung-you-w-alderman-sermon-on-christian-witness-130678.asp?Page=1

myself, I have learned one thing...If you do not move forward after a setback, you will always be "set back." You will never be who God intended you to be. Another thing that I have learned is that you must accept the reality of your setback. Whether it is a relationship that has failed, a financial setback, or a health challenge, acceptance is necessary in order to properly deal with it.

Living in denial will only intensify your pain and cause your healing to be delayed. You can come back after a setback if you confront it, thereby bringing resolution and resolve.

Here are five "A's" that can keep you moving ahead and help you overcome any setbacks in your life:

Acknowledge:
Acknowledging that something has gone terribly wrong and realizing that you need to make mid-course corrections is one of the hardest things to do, especially after a major setback. However, if you don't make changes, it could cause what is bad to become even worse...or irreparable.

Align:
When we go through tough times, it is imperative that we have the right people in our circles of influence. Align yourself with people who will encourage and inspire you out of your dark place.

Accentuate:
Accentuate the positives and minimize the negatives in your life.

Articulate:

Articulate your vision. Say it out loud. Speak positive and good things about yourself. Open your mouth and proclaim your vision.

Accelerate:

Get out of the setback as soon as you can. Do not stay there and wallow in it. Shake the dust off your feet and keep on moving. Be they ever so small, even baby steps are important. Just keep moving ahead.

Getting Back on Track

Once you are ready to make your comeback, just do it! There are many things in life that you cannot change. Accept them and move on. Change what you can! Be your authentic self! Love God and people, and enjoy life! Do not let life pass you by while you keep trying to fix things that you cannot fix, or change people that you cannot change. Find your "Happy Place" and run to it! Do not spin your wheels trying to fix what you cannot fix.

The Serenity Prayer reads:

> *God grant me the serenity to accept the things I cannot change; courage to change the things I can; and the wisdom to know the difference.*

Moving Forward From A Setback

So, you are recovering from a setback and are now ready to get back in the game. You have heard everyone's opinions, and now you must decide what is best for you. How do you get back in the game? This process can be tricky and requires that you move very strategically. It must be well thought out and you must count the cost of every decision that you make. I once had a major setback that turned out to be a tremendous "set up."

I experienced this setback while on vacation in Nashville, Tennessee. My husband, Michael, and our youngest son, Solomon, drove to Nashville to celebrate the 4th of July. We were very excited and were anticipating a fun, stress-free, uneventful time. Needless to say, this vacation was far from that. After researching the website featuring "Diners, Drive-Ins, and Dives" for a nice place to eat, we discovered that one of the restaurants was about fifteen miles away. Michael, Solomon, and I set out to visit it. It was rainy, but was still a pleasant day. Upon arrival, we were invited to sit on the porch of the restaurant to wait until there was a table available for us. While waiting to be called, I was feeling great and was enjoying the conversation of the ladies sitting near us.

After about thirty minutes, our name was called and we were escorted to our table. We were so excited about being at a restaurant featured on "Diners, Drive-Ins, and Dives." The restaurant was quaint and every inch of the homelike environment was filled. We placed our order and were given biscuits to enjoy while we waited. When our food arrived, it looked delicious and we could hardly wait to dig in. After several bites, I began to experience heart palpitations. I just knew that everyone was looking at me. My heart was beating so hard and rapidly that it felt as though it was going to jump right out of my chest. I had never had this feeling before. I excused myself and went to the restroom. As I walked into the restroom I thought I was going to pass out. The feeling of anxiety that I was experiencing grew worse. Upon returning to our table I announced to my husband that we needed to leave immediately. I tried to remain calm so as not to upset him or our son, but by this time I was really feeling bad...trying desperately to hide how ill I was.

We paid our bill and went to our car. I did not want to go to the hospital, so I tried to refocus my attention on the scenery along the route back to the hotel. It did not work. My husband knew that I was not doing well. We went back to our hotel and decided that, if I was not better within thirty minutes, we would locate and visit the nearest emergency room. After about twenty minutes in our room, I told Michael that I needed to go to the hospital. He had already selected a hospital and was trying to figure out how to get there. I was thinking to myself, "What a way to spend our vacation!" When we arrived at the hospital, we were seen right away. Anytime anyone tells the intake worker that they are having heart palpitations, they are taken back immediately. I guess that they did not know if I was having a heart attack or what; and I didn't think so, because I wasn't experiencing shortness of breath and didn't have chest pains. But I knew from the way my heart was beating that something was definitely wrong with me.

I was seen by a doctor and my heart rate and pulse were taken. They were almost twice the normal rate they should have been. I thought, "As soon as my heart goes back into normal range, I am out of here." Wrong! After seeing a cardiologist and an endocrinologist and having test after test, my diagnosis was in. It was surmised that I had gone from hypothyroidism to hyperthyroidism. This meant that my blood pressure was out of whack. It was further diagnosed that I had hypertrophic cardiomyopathy (HCM) or, in layman's terms, a "thick" heart.

HCM is a condition in which the heart muscle becomes thick. Often only one part of the heart is thicker than the other parts. The thickening can make it harder for blood to leave the heart, forcing the heart to work harder to pump blood. It also can make it harder for the heart to relax and fill with blood. HCM is also a condition that is usually passed down through families, or inherited. It is believed to be a result of several problems or defects with the genes that control heart muscle growth. Though younger people are likely to have a more severe form of HCM, the condition is seen in people of all ages. Some patients have no symptoms. They may not even realize they have the condition until it is found during a routine medical exam. The first symptom of HCM among many young patients is sudden collapse and perhaps even death. This can be caused by very abnormal heart rhythms called arrhythmias or by blockage of blood from the heart to the rest of the body.[3]

Upon hearing this diagnosis, I thought, "What is going on? Do I have a heart condition where I can drop dead at any moment?" I could not believe my ears. I was hooked up to a heart monitor, I had an IV, and I could not even go the restroom alone. As I lay there, I kept wondering what I had gotten myself into. I sincerely wished I had never agreed to come to the emergency room, especially after they admitted me. I was finally discharged after two days with three medicines in hand that I was instructed to take. Though I knew I had to take it easy for a while, I also knew that I could not allow my diagnosis to debilitate me. I was not going to allow this situation to blow my candle out. It took a while, but I finally got my strength back and began going to the gym two or three times a week. I also started speaking life to my body. I meditated on what I could do and I did not dwell on

[3] http://www.nlm.nih.gov/medlineplus/ency/article/000192.html

negativity. I did not allow myself to reiterate or keep rehearsing the doctor's diagnosis.

My experience could have been a major setback in my life had I allowed it to cripple me. It could have made me fearful and steal my dreams. But it "set me up" to take better care of my health. I encourage you to use what was meant for evil in your life to help thrust you forward in your destiny. Make a decision to move past every setback. Choose to shine!

THE OCCULERE:

Removing the Shroud of Darkness

Dr. Anya Miller Hall

They were more at home in the darkness where inky blackness kept them from seeing that which they abhorred the most. The deep shadows were like wombs in which they could nestle and find comfort and solace. It was a place where they could lick their wounds and excuse the cruel treatment they inflicted on those deemed lesser. The blackness limited their sight and kept them from genuine vision. Most of all, it served as a prison for the ones they counted as insignificant, but also greatly feared. They feared them because they carried within them a power that would expose the truth. The truth that though they were kept hidden, they were the key to everything; for within them was light, for within them was life.

For thousands of years, women have been shrouded in darkness, as men and sometimes other women sought to keep them oppressed. Using measures such as cultural norms, Biblical texts, tradition, custom, and ignorance, generations have unleashed the occult against young girls and women of all races, ages and nationalities. These women have become so accustomed to the darkness that it has become normal to them. They feel that somehow, they belong there. They have come to believe that, for whatever reason, they deserve to be there.

The word occult, or occulere`, means to conceal, hide, cover, and keep secret. For generations, women succumbed to this smothering force: dumbing down to hide their intelligence and quick wit, taking on a frumpy appearance to hide their glamorous beauty, backing down to hide their spunk and allowing their work to be stolen. They hid their ingenuity, innovativeness, and creativity.

Like a heavy mantle made of smoldering wet coal, the forces of darkness tried to stifle their light and destroy them in the process. Yes, for far too long women have been subjugated. Those brave few who have dared to stand, speak, and fight have been persecuted, openly humiliated, insulted, and discredited.

Janusz Korwin-Mikke addressed a European Parliament Session held in Brussels in March 2017. As the members of Parliament discussed the gender pay gap and how to remedy it, the seventy-four-year-old Korwin-Mikke emphatically made this statement:

> *Of course, women must earn less than men in the workplace because they are weaker, smaller and less intelligent.*

The paradox of a "successful" woman is seen in the plight of thirty-one-year-old Wu Mei (not her real name), a Chinese attorney from Beijing. In 2013, Wu earned a salary of roughly 150,000 USD per year, yet she was locked in an abusive marriage that lasted for 5 years. She was able to obtain a divorce only by relinquishing her home, her life savings, and most of her belongings. In the 2013 Spring Edition of the online magazine *Dissent*, Wu Mei was featured in an article titled "Women's Rights at Risk" by Lena Hong Fincher. Regarding her marriage, Wu Mei was quoted as saying:

"I cried every day on my drive home from work. I just wanted to escape."

These and many other incidents, including the many misogynistic comments made by the current United States president, Donald Trump, are some of the indignities that women must endure as society repeatedly attempts to cast the occulere` blanket over them.

Nevertheless, we women are rising up! Women are, and have always been, a phenomenon. Men cannot do without us. Society would likely fall apart if we were not present. Indeed, the world would be a barren place without us. Women are incredibly resilient, courageous and strong. We are intelligent and skilled warriors who have an indomitable spirit.

Consider Candace, Empress of Ethiopia. Candace was one of the greatest generals of the ancient world. She was renowned as an excellent military tactician and field commander. It is said that, when Alexander the Great reached the borders of her land during his world conquest in 332 B.C., Queen Candace personally led her army on specially trained war elephants. Not wanting to suffer a defeat that would sully his heretofore unbroken chain of victories...especially at the hands of a woman, Alexander chose not to invade Ethiopia.

Worthy of contemplation is Maya Angelou, who was raped at the age of seven, and who did not speak for five years after her assault. Yet she went on to be an acclaimed "Poet Laureate of America," as well as an actor, singer, writer, world traveler, and civil rights activist. When she reclaimed her voice, she stood in her strength and spoke clear truth to power and did so unapologetically!

Orson Welles once called this next woman "the most exciting girl in the world!"

Audiences everywhere were mesmerized by the purr of her unique and seductive voice, as well as her sultry dance moves. She spoke 4 languages and sang in seven of them. She performed on stage, on TV, and in movies. How can this be? She was the product of the rape of her African American sharecropper mother by a white plantation owner. After she was born in the cotton fields of South Carolina, her mother gave her away.

By the time she was nine, she was living in New York City. By the age of fifteen, she had dropped out of high school and lived the best that she could. She resided intermittently between the houses of friends or in the cold dampness of the underground subway system. Yet she found the strength to rise! She overcame it all! She even triumphed over being blackballed and exiled from the United States for speaking truth to power to then First Lady of the United States, Lady Bird Johnson regarding the Vietnam war. Nevertheless, she became the toast of Paris and was eventually welcomed back to the United States, apologized to, reinstated into society, and pardoned. "She" was Eartha Kitt...our very own "Catwoman," a recurring guest star on the 60's hit TV show "Batman." Like a cat, she landed on her feet every time people tried to trip her up. Women are amazing! It begs thinking about. As amazing as we are, why are we so easily held down or held back? Could it be that we feel isolated in our situation or circumstance? Could it be that we don't possess the confidence or strength of character? Maybe it's a lack of support. Or, maybe it is group thinking.

While there are matriarchal and matrilineal societies and cultures in the world where women are venerated and treated with respect, you don't hear much about them; because there are even more cultures that are dismissive, disrespectful, and outright hateful toward women.

The traditional role of women may be customary, but that doesn't mean that it is right or righteous. Women have the same potential as any man, if not more, to be responsible, productive leaders; and they should be treated as equals. Not only must men understand and embrace this truth, women must do so as well. Many women have been conditioned from childhood to subconsciously think of themselves as "less than." This lie has become entrenched in their belief system and sabotages their every attempt to break free of outdated parameters.

That is why it is imperative that we women rise up, speak up, and cast off the cloak of the occult. We must begin to tell our own stories. As we begin to read or listen to the stories of the triumphs of other women who overcame hardships, prejudices and abuse, we will realize how very strong, intelligent, beautiful and brave we are. We will no longer be kept out of the board room. We will not be muted! No longer will we allow others to take credit for our hard work while allowing ourselves to be phased out and made obsolete. We will meet and exceed every standard placed before us! We will not only reach the bar, we will leap over it!

It is imperative that we exercise the power that we have in the here and now. Women control 85% percent of the buying power in the United States. The 2015 Report of the McKinsey Global Institute states: *In a "full potential" scenario in which women play an identical role in labor markets to that of men, as much as $28 trillion, or 26 percent, could be added annually to the global GDP by 2025.* GDP stands for "gross domestic product," and is the total monetary value of all the goods and services completed within a country's borders inside a specific time period. The GDP is an indicator of a country's economic health and standard of living. Women are good for the economy! The more we women are allowed to rise and shine, using our intelligence and skill to produce need-based goods and services, the more the wage gender gap is closed. This means that the United States will become more prosperous. Consider that we women re-invest up to 90% of our earnings back into our family and communities; while men re-invest only thirty to forty percent. Is there any wonder why the family, the foundation of our society, is crumbling?

We sometimes shield our eyes from the light that could free us. It's bright, it's painful, and it is revealing. It reveals our insecurities and our many frailties. Most of all, it reveals our fear. We will remain spiritually pale and pasty and not as strong as we pretend. But after we embrace the light, we may try to reach back for the familiar cloak of the obsidian darkness that envelops us, only to realize that it is no longer there. Finally...at last...the light...the glory that shines forth so brilliantly from the unique being that is woman, pierces the gloom and causes the darkness to flee. This newly-freed woman gasps with determination as purposeful breaths fill her lungs. Corporately, she gathers strength to rise and cry with the voice of every woman that came before her, and every one that will come after: "I will be hidden no longer!"

A native of Central Florida, Dr. Anya Miller Hall is a graduate of the Jacksonville Theological Seminary. She is a Master Teacher, an Expert Facilitator, and a Certified Behavioral Analyst and Consultant. Known as "Dr. Anya," she is the Founder of TeKton Ministries International. She has traveled extensively, both domestically and internationally, in ministry. Her passion is to help people discover their value so that they can walk in their God-ordained purpose. Known as an anointed vessel and a servant leader, she is also a lyricist and has authored over forty self-published books. A devoted and loving mother and grandmother, Dr. Anya resides in the Metro-Orlando area. For more information: www.dranya.com.

SHINE SPECIAL FEATURE: YOU ARE EMPOWERED TO DO EXPLOITS

Rev. Dr. Margaret E. Benson Idahosa
Archbishop and Trailblazer

"You are empowered to do great exploits. Do you believe it? If you can believe it, you will become it!"

--Dr. Margaret E. Benson Idahosa

She is a woman of immense grace, dignity, and honor. She is filled with love and compassion for all mankind, especially children. She commands respect when she enters a room. Her voice rings throughout sanctuaries of churches, halls of universities and corridors of the hospital she oversees. She is a woman whose vision can be seen in the educational institutions that she founded. She is the Rev. Dr. Margaret E. Benson Idahosa, widow of the late Archbishop Benson Idahosa of Benin City, Nigeria. When her husband passed away, she assumed leadership of the Church of God Mission International as Archbishop.

She preaches a message of hope and healing through the power of Jesus Christ and, under her leadership, the Church of God Mission International has grown to over 5,000 churches spread across Africa, Europe, Asia, and North and South America.

"Trust in your position in Jesus," she declares. "Trust that nothing can separate you from the love of God. Trust that God will always hear you when you call; not because you teach in Sunday school or do acts of kindness. God will hear you, not because you keep the commandments (which is good), but simply because you are a son or a daughter of God. As long as you believe in Jesus, you are a man or woman of God. Start taking advantage of your position."

Dr. Idahosa recently visited Pontiac, Michigan, to dedicate the new church of her long-time confidant and trusted friend, Pastor Theresa Lee. Though Dr. Idahosa had just ended her own convocation where thousands of people attended, she wanted to be present to support Pastor Lee. That is the kind of woman, leader, and friend that she is. While in Pontiac, she spoke words of faith and confidence, encouraging Pastor Lee and all of us to believe God for more. She also shared the remarkable journey she has undertaken since she took on her late husband's apostolic mantle.

The unexpected death of her husband, at the age of fifty-nine, left Dr. Idahosa widowed and her four grown children bereft of their beloved father. Her cherished husband and soul-mate was suddenly gone to his eternal rest with Jesus Christ and his death came as a shock to everyone, because he was never sick. She often wondered how she would make it without him by her side.

"His death left an emptiness inside me that no one could fill," she reminisced. "When he was alive, I was his chief supporter. I actively prayed for and encouraged him every day. When he died, I just wanted to remain in my cocoon. I told myself after the burial that I would just recline. By then, my children were all abroad and I planned to stay with each of them for a time, then come back to Benin to check on the ministry. But God, who knows the heart of man, directed my path to where I am today."

Dr. Idahosa had every intention of not following in her husband's footsteps as a minister, let alone a pastor. He was such a tremendous force for God that she didn't think she could possibly serve the church as strongly as he did. But God and the church members helped to change her mind and her journey began.

"I was fifty-five when my better half was taken away from me; and at that point, I was not interested in the ministry. I felt my husband's shoes were too big for me to fit. But the acceptance I got from members of the church forced me on my knees, seeking God's guidance concerning the ministry. The Lord ordered my steps to move forward from where my husband stopped; and God has continued to back me in the ministry."

Her grief made it very difficult for Dr. Idahosa to move forward. However, she refused to let the enemy extinguish her light. The Holy Spirit was alive inside of her, ready to give her the predetermined plan for her life. Through communion with the Holy Spirit, she knew that she must be the one to carry the ministry forward. She would be the one to shine a light in dark places. She understood that she was the one assigned to fulfill her husband's vision, so she made a decision to keep on living. Today the vision lives and breathes, and the success of it all is far greater than anyone could have imagined.

When Dr. Idahosa assumed the leadership role after her husband died, she had two strikes against her: 1) She was a woman, and 2) She was a widow. To step into the role of a pastor is challenging for anyone, especially someone who has to replace a beloved and influential leader. It is especially difficult for women, because tradition holds that bishops and pastors are male-dominated arenas. Though Dr. Idahosa's gender was no surprise to the Holy Spirit, who calls pastors as He will, it made many traditionalists within the church uncomfortable. Knowing of the opposition to her appointment, Dr. Idahosa went to her heavenly Father for comfort and strength.

"If only people could realize that they have no limitations on earth," she exclaims. "If you don't live life to the fullest and maximize the potential that you are born with, it's because you lack knowledge. John 14:12 states: *Very truly I tell you, whoever believes in me will do the works I have been doing, and they will do even greater things than these, because I am going to the Father.* So believe me when I say, God has confidence in you!"

When God has an assignment for you, nothing and no one can stop you. Those who opposed Dr. Idahosa's appointment in continuing the legacy of her husband had no power to stop it. Her story is a testament to the power of Almighty God. Her divine appointment was part of a sovereign plan from heaven itself. Even if anyone disapproves of what God has called you to do, they will never overcome God's sovereign plan for your life. In this respect, Dr. Idahosa is a beacon of hope for women everywhere. Her bright light, tenacity and faith are testaments to the fact that any covenant with the Holy Spirit makes you unstoppable.

Various obstacles to her appointment arose from those around her. Some felt she should find another husband and settle into a quiet life. She knows all too well how some tried to compel her to take another path.

"The pressure to remarry was there, but I invited God to help me and direct my path," she remembers. "So far, He has given me the ability to be strong in that aspect. I told Him to take the desire for another man from me. I never wanted to think about remarriage. God gives me so much to do that after a hard day's work, I just go to bed. I also had no desire to remarry, because I enjoyed my late husband so much that nobody could match him. This further strengthened my resolve to remain unmarried."

Even though Dr. Idahosa had to overcome sexism and classism, she did not back down. She doubled her efforts to empower women to become good mothers, wives and instruments for end-time evangelism. She established the women's arm of the ministry called Christian Women Fellowship International (CWFI), a non-denominational body focusing on the total well-being of Christian women.

Dr. Idahosa was also instrumental in building a multipurpose facility called the Restoration Centre. The Centre has a capacity to seat more than 10,000 souls. The Centre will serve as a conference venue, office space, a skill acquisition facility and a place to rehabilitate destitute young women. Recently, a mobile medical clinic offering free medical services to rural dwellers was added. As part of the training at this facility, Dr. Idahosa is clear on her desire to help women find their voice and speak up.

"I am not asking women to usurp the authority of men, because God made the man the head of the home," she relates. "If the head of the home is doing well in terms of providing for, caring, educating, etc., then there is no need for the woman to usurp his authority."

Dr. Idahosa is equally clear that women, whether single or married, must find and fulfill the purpose that God implanted within them.

She declares emphatically: "That which God has embedded in you is important. God put you here for your home and for others in the community to enjoy and have fellowship with. Don't die with the gift which God has given you. It is okay to do your stint at home, doing what your husband loves you to do. But do not die with the gift which God has given you."

Dr. Idahosa is fond of quoting the late pastor Dr. Myles Munroe as an example of what she means.

"Myles Munroe said there is a place on this planet earth that is very rich," she says. "It is called the cemetery. The cemetery retains gifts that were buried and songs that were never sung."

Dr. Idahosa is very clear on Who she says is the source and font of all her successes.

She proudly declares: "The source of my success is God; the Holy Spirit. The first thing I do every morning is to sing love songs to God. He rejuvenates me. It is not that I don't have challenges. I just don't allow the challenges to weigh me down. So I preach to women: 'Don't let problems dominate you, dominate your problems.'"

As you have read, Archbishop Margaret Benson Idahosa is fierce! Most women and many men would cower when confronted with some of the obstacles that she overcame. Dr. Idahosa pursues her destiny, her passion and her calling on a daily basis. Do you?

Woman of God: The plan that the Holy Spirit has for you is marvelous. It is past your expectation and belief. Just believe and it shall come to pass. Don't let the enemy extinguish your fire or your passion. The enemy tried to extinguish Dr. Idahosa's candle, but his breath was not strong enough. He did not have enough wind or power to blow it out. Dr. Idahosa is filled with the power of the Holy Spirit and there is nothing that the enemy can do to stop her.

Archbishop Dr. Margaret Benson Idahosa is wife of the late Archbishop of the Church of God Mission International. Inc., The Most Rev. Professor Benson Idahosa. Archbishop Benson Idahosa is the Presiding Bishop over a ministry that has several branches and hundreds of thousands of members worldwide. She also pastors the 5,000 capacity Faith Miracle Center Church, where multiple services are held weekly. Bishop Benson Idahosa was born on the 29th of July, 1943, into the royal lineage of the Benin Kingdom. She was ordained into the ministry on the 24th of May, 1983, and consecrated Bishop on the 5th of April, 1998. This position makes her the first female Pentecostal Bishop of a ministry of this magnitude in Africa.

Together with her husband, she has preached the Gospel of Jesus Christ in more than 140 nations, covering all the continents of the world. She is not just a woman preacher, she doubles as a father and mother to many spiritual children all over the world. Her vision and mission is to "reach the un-reached," irrespective of their location, whether in the desert or rivers and creeks. Since her consecration as Bishop, she has frequently traveled to America, Europe and various parts of Africa, as well as to far-flung communities in major towns and cities...preaching, teaching, and healing the sick and afflicted. More information on Dr. Margaret Benson Idahosa can be found at: https://believersportal.com/biography-of-bishop-margaret- benson-idahosa/

To help you achieve your dreams and goals, some of Dr. Idahosa's spiritual affirmations are listed for your benefit. They can be used as your own personal declarations. Speak and meditate on them and experience the anointing of God, released through the words of this powerful woman.

INSPIRATIONAL AFFIRMATIONS

Dr. Margaret E. Benson Idahosa

I am free from bitterness; I walk in love and power. Make a conscious effort to leave bitterness behind and forgive those who have hurt you or brought you pain and sorrow. Once you do, you will experience the joy of the Lord. That joy isn't determined by your circumstances or your environment; it comes from above. I want you to understand that bitterness is like an acid; it does more harm to the container than to the person that put it inside the container. You are going to let go and let God. Rejoice and celebrate your victory! Hallelujah!

Here are some things that you may think you can't do or achieve:

- You think you can't forgive that person who really hurt you
- You believe that the business you really want to create or get into is too great for you to succeed in or manage
- You believe you don't have enough money or aren't good enough to get married

God says, if you are willing to take action...if you are willing to make that move, then His grace is available to you. Hallelujah!

I am beautiful; I am not ordinary.
This should be your constant confession. When you believe this is true, the greatness in you begins to rise.

I am glad I am a woman.

I say to all women: You are worth celebrating! No matter what you may be going through, irritate the devil by smiling and maintaining your joy; because God's joy will help you draw from the wells of salvation.

I refuse to accept negative situations as the will of God.

The devil, not God, came to steal, kill and destroy. God sent Jesus to give you abundant life and every good and perfect gift. God does not give evil and take away joy!

I am free from burdens and yokes.

Refuse to carry what Jesus has already carried. Refuse to keep yourself in the chains He has broken.

My lack of faith in some areas does not nullify the faithfulness of God.

It's time for the devil to know who the saints are. Always remember that you are a child of God and He loves you even at your worst. Take charge!

God is still in the business of giving me blessings that no one can take from me.

I pray that there will be proofs and evidences in your life to show you that God is always with you. Your miracles will be undeniable!

The God that I serve is not weak, He is not feeble, and He is not afraid. He is a mighty God.

Expect to see your mighty God working notable miracles in your life that no one will be able to deny...in Jesus' name!

I am empowered to do great exploits.

You will soon have fresh opportunities to give new testimonies about the greatness of God in your life.

God has empowered me for notable miracles.
God is set to confirm His Word concerning you with signs and wonders following. Go in His might. Amen!

I will not let challenges cause me to relent in my praise and worship of God.
Make fellowship with God a priority. Ask God to open your spiritual eyes today to clearly see the awesome power and glory of Christ in everything.

God's presence within and around me will protect me and nothing will shake me.
Don't believe the world's negativity about recession, terror or other headlines. Believe that God is with you and will never forsake you.

I declare that the government is not my source, my salary is not my source, and my family is not my source: God is!
God is your source and He will never fail you. Trust Him and follow His directions to lead you out of hard times.

As I feed my spirit with the Word of God every day, I expect to see benefits in every area of my life.
Believe that, recession or no recession, you will constantly get your daily bread from Heaven above and have all your needs met.

I believe that God will heal me from every affliction and attack of the enemy.
The Bible says that, by Jesus' stripes, you "were" healed. "Were" is a past tense word. That means there was already healing for you before the sickness came! Hallelujah! Good health is your redemptive right. Demand it!

I will be bold and operate in faith.
You are empowered with boldness to do great exploits. Study Hebrews 4:16, Proverbs 28:1, and 2 Timothy 1:7.

I will not let arrogance, pride or rebellion distract me on my journey of exploits this year; I will stay on course and trust God to help me every step of the way.
You have been through a time of shaking and are now unsure of where you stand in life and/or with God. Know that Jesus eagerly wants to reveal Himself to you; He wants you to believe in Him again.

God not only wants to equip me for great exploits, He wants to use me to equip others as well.
I pray that no one will feel powerless around you this year. I pray that anyone who has been bruised, abused, or exploited by the issues of life will find solace and strength whenever they are in your presence. God will use you to teach, train, love, and encourage others. Your light will shine to help others see themselves the way God sees them.

I will be intentional about growing and developing my leadership skills and capacity.
Remember God's directive in Isaiah 48:17 (NIV) "...I am the Lord your God, who teaches you what is best for you, who directs you in the way you should go." Remember Psalms 18:34: "He teaches my hands to war, so that a bow of steel is broken by mine arms." Declare this boldly! Amen!

I believe that God has confidence in me to do great things. I won't let my or others' low opinions of myself keep me from walking in God's Power.

John 14:12 states: "Very truly I tell you, whoever believes in me will do the works I have been doing, and they will do even greater things than these, because I am going to the Father."

I believe that God will meet me in the place that He has assigned for me. Therefore, I will not fear and I will not give up!
"It is the Lord who goes before you. He will be with you; he will not leave you or forsake you. Do not fear or be dismayed." Deuteronomy 31:8

Dr. Idahosa's Final Declaration For You:

"I declare that a strong force of Divine Favor will come upon you. God will cause men and women from far and near to single you out from the crowd and bestow favor upon you. Hallelujah!"

YOU ARE BRILLIANT: ALL YOU NEED IS A GOOD POLISH

Sima L. Ballinger, B.B.A

It is a fair statement to describe ourselves as diamonds in the rough. You and I are of great value, but sometimes in our lives we need to be refined. With the many trials, tests, and temptations that come our way, we need to know how to turn them into opportunities to shine. I wasn't always someone who shined. After an eighteen-year hiatus, I became very discouraged when I attempted to return to the workforce full-time. The dust, grit, and grime of life tried to blow out my light; but I believed I could get my luster back through some serious soul-searching. Once my internal search light was turned on, I had a change in my attitude and mindset that helped me understand I needed to do more and be more. At the age of fifty-four, I made a bold move and took on a full-time job. Please understand, as I said, I had not been employed in a full-time job in eighteen years. So, you may wonder, why did I want to get back in the workplace at this stage of my life?

My husband retired after working with a great company and having an awesome career. However, with retirement comes a decrease in cash flow and benefits. Our youngest child had entered college, and the need for my husband and I to assist him financially and help build his dream remained. The more I analyzed the future, the more I felt an obligation to step up my game to achieve this goal.

I tried my best to find a suitable part-time job and was invited to about seven interviews, but nothing good materialized. I began to question if my mature look and my gray crown were keeping me from being employed. After being called in for a second interview at the State Court, the Director of Human Resources phoned me and told me that I was "over-qualified." The conversation with this gentleman was an eye-opener. Never before had I received such advice from a potential employer. After we talked, I realized that I was aiming too low in my job search. That call from that human resource director was a pivotal turning point in my search for freedom.

During my job search, I was blessed to have good friends and family, whom I could talk with and share what I was going through. I would send an occasional email to a minister who had my best interests at heart. She always provided me with encouraging words that made me feel I could take on the challenge of giving up my freedom at home to enter a more structured professional life that would involve working from 8am to 5pm. This change was not something I was fond of at all, but I took courage and stepped out in faith.

With that being said, allow me to paint a picture of myself before I was all polished once again. I didn't work for eighteen years because I made a decision to be available to raise my three children as they were growing up. But those eighteen years out of the workplace felt like a century when I finally decided to go back to full-time employment.

Have you ever had to break through your old way of thinking in order to create a new way of thinking in your life? When I tell you it was hard for me to change, I want to emphasize the word "hard." One reason this change was hard was because of my reluctance to listen to and be coached by my husband about financial matters. He provided great advice on how to manage my money, but I didn't want to hear it, and sometimes rejected it.

During the last four years of my eighteen-year work sabbatical, I qualified to do content mill writing for a major online news outlet. Working from home is not new; but I am sure you know someone who has tried (or maybe even you have tried) to make a bundle of money while working in your pajamas. But it is difficult to make a decent wage doing content mill writing, because the competition is extremely high. However, I was in love with the idea of working from home and making money.

As a content mill writer, I would see a little dribble of cash flow into my account on the twentieth of every month. As the months went by, more dribbles of cash came in. Back then, my highest monthly earnings would be considered a real joke by today's standards. I only made $300 a month exercising my writing ability. However, I did not think it was a joke at the time; I actually thought it was pathetic. Instead of freeing me, those paltry earnings had me bound. Providing meaningful financial assistance to my family seemed out of my reach, and I felt like I was living in a dark, hidden place.

My breakthrough from that place of darkness began the day my spouse retired from his good government job. Let me tell you, this was a blessing in disguise. His presence at home freed me up to work an 8am – 5pm job, but I was afraid to step out in faith. However, knowing that our youngest child would still have support at home gave me considerable consolation. Even though I sometimes complained about the cash I did not have, in all honesty, I still had everything I needed. In fact, I had no reason to complain. I discovered that I needed to be grateful and express my gratitude for my life, my husband

and God. When I did that, boom! A bright light came on inside of me.

The reality of needing to make a major change in my life stayed with me and I earnestly began searching for a full-time job with benefits. Again, I had not worked full-time for eighteen years, so trying to find a job initially made me feel devastated, lost, and confused. Trust me, I needed therapy. My emotional state was like riding a roller coaster: one day I was up, the next day I was down. Constantly seeking motivational teaching and reading inspirational material was my mainstay. Also, YouTube™ became one of my closest companions. One day, while listening to the Tedx™ Talks on YouTube™, I came across a lady who truly inspired me. She gave a speech about throwing out the idea of needing passion to succeed.

She said, "Forget passion."

Wow! Her words really caught my attention! Her way of thinking was a relief for me and gave me the motivation I needed to accomplish my goal of getting better employment. In her speech, she said that it is okay to do different things in your life in order to make progress and enjoy life.

The statement that really drove everything home for me was when she said, "It is okay to get a job to earn a living."

She explained that there was nothing wrong with simply working in order to be able to take care of yourself. Her words soothed my doubts and calmed my fears. I wanted to reach through the computer monitor and give her a great big hug.

So, let me share my thoughts about earning a paycheck. My husband has always been the main money earner in our family. He pays all the bills, and I am grateful for the many blessings God has provided through him. Having someone there to always pick up the pieces can be both a blessing and a curse. Because I knew I could always fall back on my husband's earning power, I wasn't as motivated at first to succeed in my job quest. I needed to get away from and be delivered from this kind of thinking, because it was putting limits on my ability to change.

Another major revelation that helped me move forward was when I finally understood why I needed to make this change in my life. My major impetus for change was to be a blessing to my immediate family, friends and community. My guiding thought was: "You can do better." Also, I truly wanted to help my husband achieve his dream of business ownership. His dream became my dream.

My quest to get a job and gain financial freedom took 4 months total. Every day, I would search the internet for employment that I felt was suitable for me. Eventually, I came across a job with the State of Michigan. Though I looked at their job site often, this time I saw a job that hadn't been posted before. I located the job online and saw that the deadline to apply was fast approaching. I quickly sent my application in and the State of Michigan contacted me exactly one week from the day I submitted it.

While waiting to hear back from the State of Michigan, there was a tug-of-war going on in my head. I wondered if I really was ready to give up the freedom of a flexible schedule and get up early in the morning and be gone all day. I used to joke with my husband that I planned on telling my employer that I missed my spouse and needed to go home. Or, I said that I'd tell them that I needed to go home for a nap. When you are trying to create a new habit in your life, the struggle in your mind is very real. Letting go of what you used to do, who you used to be, and people you used to be with, takes discipline and dedication. During this period of uncertainty, Evangelist Joyce Meyers' book, *Battlefield of the Mind: Winning The Battle In Your Mind*, became a great help to me.

After I started working, it took me three long months to adjust to my new schedule. Since then, my life has changed tremendously.

As I was writing my story for this book, a tragedy shook the office where I work. At the age of thirty-six, a dear co-worker was one of five persons killed in a horrific car crash. Her loss left our entire staff broken-hearted and stirred up many emotions in all of us. She was an outstanding young woman who achieved much in her short time on earth. One major accomplishment she received was getting a top award over hundreds of other possible finalists. She was a role model who taught me a lot while we worked together; and I am consoled by the fact she had a rich, full life. One of the things she taught me was how to be a servant. She kept a plaque on her wall that read: "Be The Change." She based her life on the principle of giving, which I could relate to. My entire life is based on the principle of giving. In fact, a spirit of giving is something my father passed down to me and my siblings. It's in my DNA.

Another role model in my life is Kevin Schneiders, CEO of Educational Data Systems, Inc. (EDSI). EDSI's company motto is: "Show Up, Smile, Support." Mr. Schneiders is extremely positive in his approach to tackling problems. He often cites references from a book titled, *The Dip: A Little Book That Teaches You When To Quit (And When To Stick)* by Seth Godin. Recognizing "the dip" is knowing and understanding that you are recharging or strategizing your life in order to step into a greater position. The opposite of "the dip" is the "cul-de-sac," which refers to a dead end where you just keep moving in a circular pattern without results. The knowledge of recognizing and using the principles of "the dip" was a great inspiration to me.

I am also a huge fan of televangelist Mike Murdock. His booklet, "Wisdom Key Devotional," is phenomenal. There are 365 "Wisdom Keys" in the booklet that I bring to work with me. Most days, I read at least one of the "Wisdom Keys" to help guide my thoughts. It's a strategy I use to keep moving forward...not only in the right direction, but in a more purposeful direction. The "Wisdom Key" for May 9, 2017, was: "If you don't know where you belong, you will adapt to where you are." The "Wisdom Keys" always challenge me to live in the moment and step up my game.

Another slogan I saw on Pinterest reads: "Turning fifty should mean you've had at least thirty years of experience and now you're ready to become a mentor to help others build their dreams and live great lives."

I also came up with my own personal slogan: "If you're not giving, you're not living." That statement sums up everything for me now.

At this stage of my journey, I give thanks to God for refining my life so that I can shine. I believe that He will also do the same for you.

Sima L. Ballinger is a wonderful wife, woman, mother, and life juggler who is making a difference in her workplace and community. Sima earned a Bachelor's Degree in Business Administration from Davenport University. She is an honors graduate of the Dale Carnegie course: "Effective Speaking and Human Relations." She is employed by the State of Michigan. She assists her husband as a Social Media Customer Engagement Specialist at Hobby Town. She also worked for the University of Michigan as a Field

Researcher and for The United States District Court in Detroit. She and her husband, Marvin, have three adult children. They reside in Southfield, Michigan. She can be reached at: Simaballinger@yahoo.com

DREAM AWAKE... AND BECOME THE MIRACLE OF YOUR BRILLIANCE

Pastor Judith Cooper

"Finally, what I really want is to be happy in this moment, where the magic and miracles happen. Stay in the moment and all gifts are added as you breathe and take inspired action."

--Joe Vitale

I was happiest whenever, as a child, I could escape into my world of make-believe during my naptime. After my mother settled me down in my bed, I would rise up and peek out through the window into our beautiful backyard, visualizing all my friends gathering there. Many of these friends were imaginary, based on people in the classic movies I use to watch with momma when the weather didn't allow me to play outside. They became part of my mental scenery, my décor, my life. I imagined serving them in the backyard at their elegant tables with their fine apparel. I imagined sitting at their tables and enjoying lively conversations.

Our actual backyard was beautiful. My stepfather spent painstaking hours landscaping it with bushelfuls of colorful roses. It looked like a large canvas piece painted with intentional strokes: deep oranges, salmon, pinks, and reds. Some of the white roses were sprinkled with a little red, and the yellow roses just popped right out at you like an illuminating ray of golden sunshine. When my sister and I played together in the yard, we encountered new discoveries every day within the flower beds. We watched bees pollinate the flowers; we tried to catch butterflies; we played with the caterpillars. As a six-year-old, I often alternated between my make-believe world and my actual life. My make-believe friends fit right into the realm of my imaginary world. I was content and they were content. All of us together created a flawless world of my own making. My make-believe world was full of caring hearts, shared ideas, great communication, and loud laughter that joyfully erupted from the heart.

In retrospect, I would often meditate on why I had such an active imagination as a child. How did it come to be that I was so deeply influenced by all these scenarios fashioned from both my imagination and the classic movies I watched with my mother? All I know is that I felt free living in my imaginary world, because I could escape the darkness that wanted to pull me into despair. It was as if I was aware that my innocence, my purity, and the inherent love I had inside me needed an escape from the emotional and psychological harm that lurked within and threatened to destroy me.

One day, just before my bedtime when I was about six, I overheard a loud conversation in the living room. I hid behind the couch to eavesdrop. There were close family members on my stepfather's side of the family in the room.

My aunt kept saying: "You need to tell her! Just tell her you're not her dad."

I came from behind the couch. Instantly, the entire room got quiet and I could hear their gasps and heavy breathing.

I slowly walked over to my stepdad and sadly asked: "You're not my dad?"

I expected a loving response full of comfort and assurance. He was the man that I thought would never hurt me. He was supposed to be my protector.

He looked at me, and said sarcastically, "I've taken care of you thusfar, haven't I?"

My heart dropped. Inside, it seemed as if the petals fell off the roses. I was heartbroken, but I didn't show it. It's difficult to recall what type of metamorphic transformation overtook me. I felt alone and isolated. After that encounter, I would not put my trust in anyone. Imagine living your life being normal one day, then discovering it to be shockingly abnormal the next. The sad part of it all is that it didn't have to be so devastating...if only love and compassion were part of my family dynamic of communications.

When I asked my momma about my real father, she often responded that she didn't know his first or last name. As I developed into my teenage years, it was difficult for me to move past that family secret. I grew up being filled with rage, anger, and bitterness and I rebelled. I felt that I had been dealt the wrong hand, and my life was nothing but a bad dream. Since both of my parents worked way into the evening after we got out of school, I had to care for my siblings from the young age of nine until I was into my early teens. Because I had so many adult responsibilities at such a young age, I was often blamed by my stepfather for making wrong decisions. I felt my choices were wise ones based on the circumstances of my babysitting. However, I was often punished for expressing my thoughts or my concerns. My stepfather's insults and accusations caused me to become even more withdrawn and depressed. I felt trapped. I felt my voice was being choked. No one could hear my frustration or my cries. I wanted to be understood, not misunderstood, because I was a "mistake" that I did not cause to happen. I longed for my biological father and wanted to know him personally.

I survived and struggled to stay free in my mind by finding hope in my creative endeavors, in my imaginative spirit, and in creative self-expression. I wrote poetry, listened to the Motown sound, kept a journal, and wrote in my diaries. I fed my mind by reading Life Magazine, Playboy articles and Jet Magazine. I entered storytelling contests sponsored by Readers Digest.

Though I didn't feel I was heard at home by my parents, I discovered that my struggle was compatible with what was going on in America at the time, particularly as it related to the deaths of Dr. Martin Luther King Jr., President John F. Kennedy, and Malcolm X. One thing that strongly influenced me was the Afrocentric ideas my stepdad introduced us to: wearing an afro, donning a dashiki, and embracing the cause of Black Power. This was my attempt to liberate myself in order to gain control of my identity and to have a voice. This was a movement I could get behind! I would watch television to listen to Angela Davis' enunciations in her speech and conversation. I identified with the Black Panthers, a nationalist and socialist organization who promoted the ideology of self-defense. I related to the Panthers' demands for self-respect and feeding children in the community. I was in awe of their beliefs and loved how they stood against injustice. I felt I had a calling like theirs within my free-spirit and soul; I just had to find it.

> *"Act the way you want to be and soon you'll be the way you act."*
>
> *--Les Brown*

At some point in my senior year in high school, I decided to run for Class Treasurer. The hallways were buzzing with other candidates who also thought of running for office. I meditated on it a bit, and decided that I would run. I felt I had good people skills and enough influential power to lead teams in raising money for our senior graduation activities. I took pen to paper and began to write my speech. I practiced in the front of the mirror. I practiced in front of my stepdad, and I began to visualize myself making my speech in front of hundreds of students in our school auditorium. When election day finally came, I vividly recall how each competitor walked up to the podium to give their most persuasive speech. It was so quiet in the auditorium as each person spoke. As I waited my turn, I had butterflies in my stomach but I kept my posture and composure strong. The moderator made sure that we felt comfortable by giving each of us an encouraging smile. It was finally my turn. She announced my name. It seemed like it took me forever to walk to the podium. I laid my paper down on the flat surfaced podium and looked directly out into the auditorium and proceeded with a smile:

"Dear fellow classmates. My name is Judy Larkins. I am running for office to become your next Class Treasurer."

As I began to speak, I knew I had captured the ear of my audience. I could feel their excitement. I spoke with clarity. The exact wording of my speech leaves me, but at the end I thanked them for their consideration in electing me. I then folded up my speech and returned the microphone to the moderator. As I did so, I heard loud applause. I looked out to see students standing on their feet and shouting my name for me to be elected! I was in awe of the reception my classmates had toward my speech. Their belief in selecting me from among a good panel of other students made an impression on me. Before I spoke, I was unsure of the type of response I would get. I was sure I was going to lose, but their enthusiastic response helped build my confidence and gave me the tenacity to move forward.

> *"Your visions will become clear only when you can look into your own heart. Who looks outside, dreams; who looks inside, awakes."*
>
> *--Carl Jung*

I want to examine how we can find and keep our resilience...to live with more boldness and brilliance as women. I believe there are four ways to do this: believe your miracles can happen; believe you are a unique person; believe you deserve the right to see yourself the way you want to be; and consider your heart.

Each one of us possesses passion within us. It is this passion that will cause us to be bold and see our brilliance uncovered through the power of miracles. It was an unexpected move for me to run for a school office, but my passion for people uncovered characteristics of my personality that gave me the confidence that I could make others happy and feel a part of their lives. It's your inner brilliance that wants to shine by expressing your truth with hope and optimism, two things that can protrude through the dark areas of your life.

I believe when you are called by God, you are a unique creature...having an ordained responsibility to renew, transform and bring out the uniqueness in others. I never thought God would use me in a higher calling to preach His word. I never imagined that He would use me to deliver a message on the day my stepfather walked to the altar to accept Christ. In fact, when he came to the altar, I was shocked and in disbelief. I hadn't even finished speaking. He just stood there with his hands in front of him, waiting patiently for me to say something. I finally heard God say, "Go to him."

When I stepped down to approach him, he said, "I want to be saved."

I was ecstatically overjoyed and full of tears. You see, at the age of thirteen, when I gave my life to Christ, I asked God to give me a heart to forgive my stepdad for his critical behavior toward me. My prayer was answered many years later and he became a faithful partner of our church. The presence of our uniqueness should shine so bright that it compels those we know to be drawn toward it.

You must believe that you deserve the right to see yourself the way you want to be. When I understood the gifts and callings on my life, I made it a mission to intentionally select the kind of people I wanted to engage with...those who would help me learn skill sets that lined up with my own personal interests.

Finally, consider your heart. Ask yourself: Who do I need to forgive...from my past, my present, or even in my future? If I had kept unforgiveness in my heart toward my stepdad and mom, I may have never met my real dad, nor ever discovered that he was an ordained pastor. I would have missed out on having the opportunity to meet my other siblings, and find an entirely new family heritage of people who lived right in my state. We'll never know God's miracles if we let others dim our light. I was made whole after meeting my biological father; and though he has passed away, the love I carry in my heart for him still resonates to this day.

I thank God for sharing with me the essence of His beauty during those years in my make-believe world as a youngster. His Grace helped me look at the beauty of others and forgive them. The essence of God's wisdom allows us to grow through seasons from the seeds He plants within us. Just as with my stepfather's rose bushes, God has created us to bloom through various experiences, trials, and tribulations. He has planted in us the ability to connect to everything living and to speak boldly with authority.

I can return and open my gate to gaze upon the majestic glow of roses and ponder until my heart is content. Now it is your time to smell the flowers. Light the world with your authentic self and hide no more!

Pastor Judith Cooper is an ordained minister and a certified Executive Business Coach for women entrepreneurs, strategizing their success through their personal life story and bringing out their Exceptional You! She has a social media group for women, entitled Brains, Beauty, Brands and Bangles (B4Bangles), which helps women find success in a multiplicity of business, professional, and style management venues. Judith was raised in Detroit, Michigan, and has always been interested in business development and leadership. She also has interests in organizational culture, entrepreneurial efforts, and lifestyle management within the fashion industry. As a former pastor's wife and psychotherapist, she has ministered and counseled countless women, couples and children into a place of peace and reassurance. Judith attained double masters' degrees: from Ashland Theological Seminary in Pastoral Counseling and Capella University in Management of Leaders in Nonprofit Organizations. For more information on how to contact Judith personally, please email her at: mzjudith007@gmail.com, or https://www.linkedin/in/iamjudith1.

HIDDEN FRUSTRATIONS

Pastor Regina Burrell

Something very powerful happened as I was preparing to write for this anthology. As I began to reflect over my memories, something unlocked inside of me. I had not really considered talking about the past much, because that is just what it is...the past. Writing is one thing, but being transparent about life's hard places is totally different. The freedom I encountered through writing this piece was amazing. I am so grateful to have accepted this challenge, and I hope you are as blessed by reading it as I am by sharing it.

As a teenager, I was confronted with a circumstance that could have hung a shadow over my entire life. Thankfully, I overcame this trial by God's grace and through my faith in Him.

Recently, a dear friend made a statement about me not being very trusting when it comes to other people.

I thought for a minute and very candidly replied: "You are right. I am still working on some things in my life."

But her comment caused me to look to my past. As I did so, I began to remember how the seeds of mistrust first took root in me.

For most of my adult life, it has been very hard for me to trust others. But until my friend's observation, I had never reflected on what could have happened to me that caused me to be so skeptical of other people.

I grew up as a church girl, the daughter of a pastor. We were taught according to what we believed the Bible said. No matter where we were, our family tried to live the life we were taught about in the church building. Of course there were many things that we couldn't do growing up; and I must admit I was curious as to what possible joy and fun I may have been missing, especially as a teenager. I remember wanting to "fit in" with other girls who were my age or older. However, I found that I was very different than they were.

When I had an opportunity to be close to one of the most popular guys around, I thought it would be fun. (We really didn't call what we did "dating" back then.) His father was a pastor as well, so there we were...two "Pastor's Kids" (also known as "PK's). Great, right? I thought so at the time. He was kind, but a bit elusive. However, since we were young and he was so popular, I didn't think much of it. He stayed very busy most of the time, but then, so did I. (Thinking back on that time, I remember how the older folk used to say, "If I knew then what I know now...") He and I didn't spend a lot of time with each other, but the time we had together was fun and often joyous. Because our parents all knew each other, it helped make our visits flow easier. There would be times when we didn't see each other for weeks. But we both usually had good reasons for this...and he would always call during these separations. I also received many letters from him. Sometimes they would come every day. When I read them, his words seemed to make our relationship grow stronger. Those letters made me see him as a really good friend.

One day I received a letter with his handwriting and was excited as usual, thinking it was from him. To my surprise it wasn't. As I began reading, something was revealed to me in that letter that I did not expect. It turned out to be a letter of confession. As I read this letter, I was so surprised to find out that "he" actually hadn't written many of the letters that I had received during our correspondence. In the letter, his sister was asking me to forgive her. She admitted writing to me, pretending to be her brother. (Their handwriting was very similar.) When I discovered this, it brought tears to my eyes. As I continued to read, I felt much worse than I could ever admit to myself. She was saying that it was a cruel joke she had decided to play. WOW! Some emotional and psychological adjustments had to be made on my part. Not wanting to face the reality of what was happening, I hid the way I felt from myself. I had to keep my cool as well as my reputation. I had to sort out my feelings. Here I was, thinking I was in a real relationship; but all along I was being duped. I was deeply hurt and angry to no end. I could never convey to anyone the pain, shock and disappointment that I felt. His sister's ruse created a dark space in the place where I held my truth. I decided then that this would be forever my secret. I would never show how I really felt. This frustration would be hidden within me forever. At least, that's what I thought at the time. Trying to forget something you never even wanted to admit sounds like an oxymoron. But at the time, that's how I thought of the situation. My decision to bury this disappointment resulted in years of bottled up frustration.

Hidden frustrations can be used to hinder you from your future if you allow it. You may go through many things before you realize that the one thing or opportunity that you want the most isn't meant for you. When you are bound by frustrations, you cannot enjoy the opportunities in life that you are meant to enjoy. Hidden frustrations will cover hidden potentials and disallow the plans God has for you. When you are focused on the cause of the frustration, you can miss your favorable time of progression. Letting go of broken dreams and hurt feelings will get you back on the path to your destiny.

When I looked back over my life, I realized that all the frustration and bitterness I had suffered over the years began with this one, wounding incident. After it happened, I said that I would forgive her. I made the decision to do so, but I didn't really know how. I felt rejected and alone. The thing about rejection is that it often does not present itself for what it is...it hides in other emotions. It can cause insecurity and fear. It can shut you down. Through the years, if left unattended, rejection can turn into bitterness, which can often show up in your life through other issues.

As I look back now, I can remember many times when I was unable to befriend someone because of my trust issues. Suspicion would creep in and I was unable to let people get close to me. For many years, I didn't know what it was that made me feel so insecure and untrusting. But now, I can see the source that caused all my frustration. Although I didn't realize why I was so sensitive about certain situations, I did know that I had experienced a strong sense of betrayal because of that letter episode. Thinking of that girl's duplicity often caused me to feel like I wanted to give up. However, quitting was not an option. As I grew older, trusting others was still a challenge for me; but I always knew there was a purpose for my life and I had to move on. I knew I couldn't give up, couldn't give out, and couldn't just throw in the towel. So I didn't. At some point, we all must deal with unresolved issues, and it's so important to know how. No matter what we go through, we must be determined to never be stopped or blocked by disappointments.

In recent years, I have been blessed to serve with my husband at the Praise Temple Evangelistic Church in Desoto, Texas (DFW area). Because of what I went through in my youth, I have been able to coach others who want to move from frustration to the expectation of God's best for their lives. If you have been hurt by situations in your past, I encourage you to push through to your tomorrow. As long as you have breath, you can still choose whether to be stifled and withdrawn, or to forgive, live, and move on. Forgiveness is an ongoing process that will help you live a life of freedom. It is powerfully transforming when you can recognize the darkness you've been through, and yet you're able to look back and not be bitter. Forgiveness is the key.

The other day I was reading how diamonds create sparkling displays of light. It turns out that they begin by looking dark and rough, but then must be formed with high temperatures and strong pressures deep within the earth. After they go through the process of being cut and polished, their many facets act as tiny mirrors that create the most beautiful display of light. You may go through darkness in your life, but I encourage you to push through. Remember that, as with diamonds, the pressure that you may be going through will ultimately help refine and reflect your light. There is light after your process. There is light in your future...and I hope you shine!

Regina Gant Burrell, the Pastor of Praise Temple Evangelistic Church in DeSoto, Texas, is a woman on fire for God. She is known as an "electrifying prophetess, evangelist, and songstress with a golden voice." Born and raised in the charismatic movement, Burrell overcame many who doubted her ability to lead as a woman in ministry. She surmounted every obstacle through her undeniable spiritual gifts and is one of the top female leaders in her field. She is a power broker, training and ordaining hundreds of men and women as ministers and elders. Her networking initiative to build families is changing communities at multiple levels. Pastor Burrell lives with her husband and leadership partner, Bishop Terence Burrell, in DeSoto, Texas, and they are the proud parents of one son.

ALL THE NAYSAYERS, HAVE A SEAT TO THE LEFT!

Rev. Arnita M. Traylor

We will be faced with challenges, trials, tribulations, and temptations in our lives. We may also encounter people I call naysayers and dream snatchers. They are specifically placed in our lives to discourage us from reaching our goals, dreams, and purpose. Despite what these naysayers and dream snatchers tell us, we can, by faith, conquer our destiny. Such was my experience.

I grew up in a family of eleven, the first girl after three boys. Needless to say, I was the apple of my daddy's eye and a carbon copy of my mother. My father was a barber/preacher and my mother was a housewife. My parents struggled to make a better life for us up north than we had in the south.

As a preacher's kid, I was brought up in a strict environment in the Motor City, also known as Detroit. Our lives revolved around church from Sunday to Saturday like many other families: Baptist, Pentecostal, Methodist, and other faiths. Our family was Baptist bred, Baptist fed, and Baptist led.

Worship was always spiritually energizing. I loved the music, the fellowship, the Baptist Training Union (BTU), and hearing my daddy preach. Wow! Daddy could preach until the roof would seem to open up. I knew, through his expounding on the Word of God and his teaching, that Jesus loved me...that I was so special. I knew that I could do anything my heart desired. I gave my heart to Jesus and was dipped in the water at baptism. When I came up out of the water, I remember being engulfed in a bright light and feeling immense joy. It would be years later before I fully understood what had taken place. But on that day, I knew something bigger had happened and my life would never be the same again.

As a young girl, I admired a woman preacher who led a spiritualist church around the corner from our house. She was described as an "enchanter," and wasn't considered to be a traditional preacher. Because of her reputation, we were not permitted to visit her church. Unbeknownst to my parents, I would defiantly sit outside her church to hear what was going on. I enjoyed listening to the animated worship...hearing the drums pounding, the organ blaring, the strumming guitars, and the loud shouts of jubilation. I was curious, but I never went inside. Listening to this woman preacher's services made me realize that her church culture was vastly different from ours, because she was the leader of her congregation.

When I was growing up, it was customary for a preacher to stand in the pulpit and bring the word. But that custom only applied to male preachers. When women preached at our church, they were not allowed in the pulpit. Women had to preach from either the floor or the choir stand.

One woman who was relegated to the floor became my mentor. Through her urging and prophecy, I knew that God had set me apart, and that I would impact the lives of many. She served as a strong force in mentoring me in other areas of church life. From her, I learned about using radio as a ministry tool and about community choirs. She also opened my eyes to understanding how other denominations flourished where women pastors presided and used their voice for God.

When I was eleven or twelve, I used my voice during a church meeting. The members, deacons, and trustees decided to challenge my daddy's pastorate and decision-making process. It seemed as if they all teamed up against him. Yet, none of them were avid givers or financial supporters of my father's vision. I cannot recall the main topic of discussion, but I understood from their tone that the congregation had sided against my dad. Their dissatisfaction with my father's leadership made it evident that they were going to do him in. I don't know what prompted me, but I got up as a heated debate was raging. Out of nowhere, I began to speak with authority and power and BOOM! You could hear a pin drop; a hush came over the church. Shortly thereafter, the meeting ended. A few weeks later, the disgruntled deacons resigned, but out of loyalty to my dad, the members stayed.

I realized then the power I had within me to speak God's Word. As I continued my life's journey to ministry, I more fully realized the restrictions placed on women preachers. It seemed that male preachers were free to do whatever they chose to do. I was conflicted...did God love men more than women? Because women were not allowed to preach from the pulpit, I wondered why God gave me all this mouth if He wanted me to remain silent and bound and tied to speaking from the floor? In other areas of my life, I was taught that I could do or be anything I chose to be. Why then, was I not allowed to preach from a pulpit?

God did not immediately answer my question. Time moved on and I experienced life in the fast lane. I got married and had children. But through it all, I still felt God's call on my life to preach.

Life met me with many challenges along my way to becoming the woman God created me to be. Over time, my marriage failed. I felt, at the time, that it failed because the men I knew seemingly wanted passive and submissive wives. I was neither. I was highly assertive and never afraid to speak my mind. I was an authority on everything, or so I thought. I could be soft, loving, and submissive; but I, in no way, was a weakling or person with nothing to say. When people said I could not do or be something, I would go the extra mile to prove them wrong.

My dad was a staunch believer who also told me that God did not call women to preach. This wasn't just his belief, it was an assertion etched in my spirit by many other male preachers. Even other women told me that the pulpit wasn't meant for a woman. They felt that a woman's place was behind a man.

All the naysayers have a seat to the left!

Daddy was getting up in age. He was tired and worn. Pressure in ministry does that to those who are watchmen on the wall. One Sunday afternoon in the spring of 1990, I decided to check on him because he had suffered a stroke. Though limited in his movement, he was still preaching. I called him and we chatted for a bit. I asked him what he preached that morning. He indicated a scripture that I can't remember specifically.

But I said, "Let me turn there." I opened the Bible and expounded on the Word.

When I finished, my dad asked, "Arnita, you've been called to preach?"

I immediately retorted, "No, Daddy. But when and if the Lord calls me, I know how you are about women being in your pulpit. I don't need your pulpit to preach. I will stand on the floor and tell people what thus says the Lord."

To this statement my dad said, "Uh-huh, you have been called to preach."

Then he asked me to pray for him. Never in my life had my dad asked me to pray for him.

"I do pray for you, Daddy," I told him.

He said, "I know. But I want you to pray for me now."

So I prayed. When I was finished he said, "Thank you."

Wow! What a moment. Talk about God's "Amazing Grace."

That exchange with my dad caused something miraculous to happen. There was a shifting in my spiritual atmosphere. I had been questioning my call. I struggled with the church being adamant about the role of women preachers. I agonized over being perceived as a radical, an outcast, an undesirable. But after that conversation with my father, what people thought mattered less to me. I started earnestly studying the Bible every moment I could. I inhaled the Word. The Spirit of God was teaching me how to discern the spirit of people. I began to learn how to discern healthy and unhealthy alliances. Along the way, He put people in my life who helped me develop my calling.

When my father died the following year, I knew his prophetic mantle would fall on one of my brothers. The Spirit of God gave me a prophecy that my brother would be called to preach. When I told him what God said, he didn't act on the prophecy. When he didn't accept the prophecy right away, God called me to preach. This was a defining moment for me, though I didn't fully understand what had taken place until a couple of years later. So, I continued to ignore the signs of being called to clergy ministry.

On February 17, 1993, I finally got sick and tired of battling who I was, and I acknowledged my call to preach. That day, I was alone in my office at work. Everyone else had left for the day. I heard someone call my name.

"Arnita, I called you to preach." The voice resonated throughout the office.

I thought I was hearing things. I got up to see who had come in because I knew everyone had gone for the day. I checked every room on my floor but found no one.

I heard the voice again, "Arnita, I called you to preach!"

I responded to God's Voice, but I felt a need to remind Him that I was a woman. I told Him that I did not know His word well enough. I gave God excuses. Sometimes customs, traditions, naysayers, and dream snatchers can make you miss your calling. God's response to all my excuses was: "I called you! I know who you are! I made you!"

After hearing this firm statement, I reverently replied, "Your servant hears, Lord. I will obey. I will preach."

Peace and joy encompassed my whole being. I cried tears of joy and had to tell somebody. I called my mom and told her what had just taken place. It was not a surprise to her, and she began to rejoice and cry with me. We had a Holy Ghost praise party! I then remembered that daddy had asked about me being called to preach. God revealed my calling to my dad before he passed on to his heavenly reward.

Leaving work, I could not wait to tell my husband my news...but I was also nervous. Though I was happy to receive God's call, I did not know what my husband's response would be once I told him. Before we were married, he told me he did not want a woman who was never at home. He didn't want his wife running here and there all the time.

When he came to pick me up from work, I told him how I had been called to preach. I acknowledged that I knew he had not asked for a preacher-wife when we got married. I told him that if he wanted out of our marriage, there would be no hard feelings. My husband told me that he already knew that I was called and said he would support me. Thankfully, for about eleven years he did. But when I went back to school to better equip myself for ministry, things changed. He taunted me when I retired from work so I could do full-time ministry. My husband would take my computer away from me and accuse me of having affairs with other male preachers. There were many days when he would verbally demean me right before I had to preach. Ultimately, he decided that he wanted no part of the church or my ministry.

I endured my husband's constant verbal abuse for years before I asked the Lord to help me. I had taken the marriage vow: "Through good times and bad...in sickness and health...for better or worse." But God does not expect us to be a whipping post or an abused doormat. This was not God's perfect will for me; and, if you are in an abusive situation, it is not His will for you. Sometimes your enemy is not without, but within.

As a result of my issues with my husband, my health was affected. I was so distressed that my skin turned scaly and dark. I tried not to reveal my problems to anyone. I was smiling on the outside, but my insides were dying.

Finally, I sought God's wisdom as to what I should do about my situation. I told God I felt my husband's behavior was a hindrance.

God questioned me: "Are you going to be satisfied if I move him?"

"Yes, Lord, I will be satisfied."

The final straw came as I was preparing to move into the parsonage of a new church. We had our own house, but he told me I was not welcome there. Amazingly, as I was moving into my new parsonage, he decided he wanted to move with me. I truly did not want him to come. Before my move, I sent some furniture to be refurbished by a local upholsterer. The upholsterer's store caught fire and all my furniture was consumed. The fire did more than burn my furniture; it burned what was left of my marriage. After the fire, my husband told me he wanted nothing more to do with me. He told me that I was a good pastor and minister, but he no longer wanted to be married to a preacher. He gave me the keys to our house and left. We agreed to divorce. I have not heard from him since the day of the divorce, and I am at peace with God's intervention.

Many years have passed since finding my voice. I have experienced life in many facets: as a young girl speaking in my father's church; singing in community choirs, night clubs, piano bars, stage productions, and even the White House. Every step of my journey prepared me to be a pastor and overseer of souls.

If you are wrestling with what you have been called to do, just keep listening. Continue to follow the voice and strong urging within you. There is a process in getting to your destiny. What you are going through is not meant to kill you, but to mold and shape you into who you are meant to be.

You are called to do a great work, but you must be willing to trust the process. If your call is to ministry, God will equip and ordain you.

To know your true purpose, be bold and strong. Trust that all things are working out...not just for your best, but for your "better." Let the light within you dispel the darkness around you.

Today, I am a woman who is unapologetic in who I am as a mother, a teacher, a leader, and a charismatic. I realize that God has always been with me and shaped me into who I have become. God will be with you, too. I no longer apologize for who I am and how God made me. I praise God for delivering me from doubt to certainty. I am fearfully and wonderfully made in God's image. I am a vessel called to proclaim the Good News with integrity to those in darkness and fear. I am an instrument shaped by God. I will use His power to change lives, heal hurts, and restore hope...because of the light that shines within me.

So, to all the naysayers, have a seat to the left.

Rev. Arnita M. Traylor is an ordained Elder in the African Methodist Episcopal Church (AMEC) and a Senior Pastor, St. John AME in River Rouge, Michigan; the first female pastor in ninety-nine years. She has served over fifty years in ministry, nineteen of which were served in pastoral ministry in the United States and Canada. This mother of three sons, fourteen grandchildren and one great-grandchild holds a B.S. in Business Administration and an M.A. in Pastoral Ministry. She has served in various capacities: VP of Downriver Interdenominational Ministerial Alliance (DIMA); AME North District Social Action Commission Chairperson; AME Southeastern Ministerial Alliance Recording/Financial Secretary; St. John Hospital-Clintondale Clinical Health Systems Board Member. Arnita Traylor has gifting in music, prophecy, discernment, healing, teaching and preaching. Her mantra is to preach Christ and..."Change lives! Heal hurts! Restore hope! Initiate love! Save souls! Trust God!"

Contact info: St. John AME Church in River Rouge, MI

TRAVELING GRACE

Rev. Helene M. Walker

Living life can be compared to traveling on a road. We enter onto the highway and, after a time, we exit the highway. We have a beginning of life and, after a time, an ending of life. What we do in between makes the difference. Some parts of the road are smooth driving and some parts are rough. Life is the same way. There are detours and potholes that you must watch out for because they can change the direction that you are trying to go. You must watch out for reckless drivers and pedestrians...just the same as you would the people in your life. I entered this lifelong highway on a rough road as a timid little girl.

The little girl that I used to be is different from the woman that I am now. She was timorous with little confidence in herself. She wore bifocal glasses; she had short hair and a very bad complexion. She was very skinny and wore very cheap, plain-looking clothes. Her parents never had a real relationship; they were just two young people who had had a sexual encounter.

Her uncle teased her saying: "When your mother told your father she was pregnant with you, he told her he was going to buy a pack of cigarettes...and he never came back."

The little girl I was didn't meet her father until the age of seven and she only saw him about three more times after that. You can say that she entered life on the rough road. Her mom was very bitter and sad about life, because she didn't think life was fair to her. It is very difficult for me at times to remember myself as the little girl I was. That little girl suffered so much pain and felt so unloved by her mother. My mother cussed me out a lot and called me unpleasant names. She told me that I was going to be just like my father...a "nobody!" Her words scarred me badly and I hated the way she talked to me. I never felt like she loved me. I think it was because of what my dad did to her. I tried to escape it all by taking my life. I swallowed a lot of pills and lay down to die; but God kept me from dying. I left home early and married my childhood boyfriend to get away from it all, but that only made matters worse. We were teenagers with children and he was physically abusive. I tried to committee suicide again, and again God saved me. I was on a very bumpy road, caught up in the worse storms of my life. There was always a feeling of loneliness, hopelessness, and despair.

The concept of each of us traveling along life's highway was brought to mind as I thought about my own life's journey of grace. We must learn to look at life with a positive mindset, no matter what difficulties we face. We must look at the glass as half-full and not half-empty. My troubled childhood and bad marriage made me stronger. Although I had many challenges, those two were the major challenges in my life. I've learned to evaluate them and work through them and not give up.

I didn't let my setbacks hold me back. I went back to school and finished my education while I was still working and raising small children. It was the most difficult time of my life. It seemed like all I was doing was driving in and out of storms. People did not want to give me a break; I had to work hard for all my accomplishments. Getting a decent education was the core of getting my life back on track. I was working from sun up until sundown. Being a single mom while working and going to school was not a smooth ride. But, I pressed forward with a made-up mind, knowing that God was going to help me have a better life.

Traveling life's highway is full of interesting experiences, some good and some bad. When you are traveling along the real highway of life, you have to pay attention to the road or you will hit potholes, run into ditches, or have accidents that set you back and keep you from reaching your destination safely. I have learned to watch out for other drivers and to be careful when the weather is bad, because it makes traveling difficult. Real-life highway conditions are comparable to situations in your personal life that can happen if you make bad decisions. My beginnings might have been rough, but as I made better decisions, my life got easier. A better education meant a better job. I went from being on welfare to working at a law office. I learned to not let what people say or think about me define me. I used the hurtful words I heard as stepping stones to continue on my journey of grace. The pain brought me to my knees, but closer to God. Life's pains taught me how to pray and gave me traveling grace. I cried and pleaded with God and He heard my cry. God gave me purpose...and that was to live for Him and do His will. I learned to depend on God and nobody else. The little girl in me had grown up strong in the Lord and was not afraid to face life's challenges.

Today, I am a strong woman in the Lord, and I let God be my Guide on this highway of life. He has helped me to make better decisions. I am married again and my children are all grown up. Now that my children are adults with their own families, I have more time to listen to God, to pray to Him, and to meditate. Being able to shine is really all about helping others. Isn't that what Jesus did while He was on His life's mission of saving souls? Helping others takes me away from focusing too much on my own problems. Helping others gives me joy...especially when I see someone who felt like giving up begin to live life again to the fullest.

I have been traveling down this highway for a while and the roads are getting smoother. I've learned that we still must pay attention to all the signs on the road, because Satan tries to travel with us. He is always straying into our lane...constantly trying to deceive us. I thank God for His angels, who protect us all from dangers on life's actual and personal roads. Angels are those people who encourage, support, and give us aid. You must be careful who you let into your inner circle, because they can either encourage you or destroy you. I thank God for the power of prayer and endurance. I thank God for patience and understanding. There are a lot of things that seem impossible, but they "are possible" with the help of our Savior. God has blessed me with what seemed impossible. I have been working all my adult life at good-paying jobs and I only have two years to go before I can retire. God has taken me from living in the projects to dwelling in a beautiful, quiet neighborhood. He has blessed my children with decent jobs and families of their own. I now have many testimonies to share and encourage others when I preach, teach, or talk to friends and relatives about the goodness of God. Our life testimonies are our best witnessing tools, not fancy sermons.

One area in my life of which I am the most proud is being a United Auto Workers (UAW) chaplain. At first, I was not sure how to be a chaplain. I felt like I was riding down a highway in the fog, not being able to see clearly. I started with little or no directives. A man in the plant where I worked heard about the virtue of integrity that I try to live. He was a man of power and authority in the UAW and offered me a position that I had never encountered. He entrusted me with building a chaplaincy program under his watch. Words cannot express how I felt about being tasked with such a great honor. There was a lot of work to be done to begin my new adventure, but I was still excited. I had to create a plan, since I was given no training and had no roadmap to follow. I was the first appointed chaplain in my building. I am so grateful for God, who guides us along life's highway. God speaks to us as He whispers in our ear, when He opens doors of opportunity, and when He guides us by His spirit and sends angels to assist us. We simply need to always be listening, watching and waiting for His instructions. When you have a good and healthy prayer life, and when you spend quality time in the Word of God, you give the Holy Spirit something to work with. The Spirit of God was my teacher in this new assignment.

The UAW is a very structured organization. Once I learned how the chaplaincy program fit into that structure, with the help of the Holy Spirit, I had a foundation to build upon. There were a few people who tried to show me shortcuts just to gain power and position and/or get doors open for me...but I chose to follow God and do it His way.

The UAW and the chaplaincy program both have three divisions: International, Regional and Local. Once I learned how the Chaplaincy Program operated, it was time to meet the people that I was called to serve. (Just as in life, once you learn to drive, it's time to get on the highway.) Meeting and communicating with people can be like riding next to other cars on the highway. They come in all colors, sizes and styles. They drive all kinds of ways in all kinds of vehicles. Some are rude and some are polite. Some are easy to work with and some are not. But in spite of it all, I still love being a chaplain.

The Chaplaincy Program holds an annual meeting in Black Lake in Onaway, Michigan, at an educational center owned by the UAW. Chaplains meet there to participate in a conference for training, instructions, and inspiration. My first visit was very exciting. The conference continued for one week. It went from morning until night and the main topic was God. Being at that conference felt somewhat like heaven to me. All day long, we did nothing but learn about God and praise Him. He was the topic of all our conversations. I was on a spiritual high. The reason this was so important to me was because most of the conference attendees worked in factories, where the atmosphere is oftentimes unpleasant and ungodly. People working on the shop floor have a different way of dealing with each other than people working in a more professional atmosphere. There is a lot of stress on the shop floor and I try to stay away from the everyday drama. Therefore, the Chaplaincy Conference at Black Lake was a refreshing change. It was like driving down a cloudy highway before suddenly seeing the sun come through to shine very brightly. It was so pleasant to be in that conference with likeminded people. They were like angels placed by God in my life to help me on my journey of grace.

I am so glad that I decided to trust God on my life's journey of grace. Life is never easy without God. Throughout my life, I had always helped other people fulfill their dreams but had neglected my own. Early in my life, God had given me a path to follow, but I didn't have the faith to pursue it because I didn't believe in myself. Now, as I travel my journey of grace, I feel more confident. I am now the founding pastor of Realistic Ministries Church, and we celebrated the works of God at our first church service in January 2017. Realistic Ministries Church is built on God's Word. Our goal is to always strive to be a healthy church...not a megachurch or a popular church, but a healthy church. We believe that a healthy church is a church that loves God and His people unconditionally. A healthy church is a church that knows the real enemy is Satan. A healthy church is filled with followers and disciples of Jesus Christ, the Son of the Living God. A healthy church believes, studies, and lives by God's Holy Bible.

As I write this, I am entering my senior years and I feel great. I am coming near the end of my earthly road with no regrets. My journey of grace is very rewarding. God has given me some great rewards already, both personally and spiritually. And, because of my hard labor as a chaplain at Ford Motor Company, they have acknowledged the role of the chaplaincy program in the UAW-FORD National Contract. This was a victory for all those who labor in chaplaincy. Also, as expressly stated in our local contract, I now have a chaplaincy room named after me as well as a private parking space. I have implemented a first-time chaplaincy manual for our local shop that outlines the chaplaincy program within the UAW. The manual serves as a guideline for us all to follow so that we are in one accord.

I know that one day I will have to exit this highway of life. But while I'm still traveling, God is causing me to shine; and I am so grateful for all He has done. I used to be afraid of driving on real-life highways, mainly because I got lost easily and I was afraid of large trucks. The rude drivers were also intimidating to me, and I did not like the feeling of being vulnerable on dangerous roadways. We must never be afraid to step forward in faith or we might miss out on some of the wonderful opportunities and blessings that God has for us. I am no longer afraid to travel on life's real highways, and I look at my life challenges with confidence. I know that, if a poor girl from the projects can make a difference, anybody can. We are not blessed because of what we know, who we know, or who we are. My childhood pastor told me that God is looking for "F.A.T." Christians who are: Faithful, Available, and Trainable. We are blessed, because God blesses "F.A.T" Christians. I have always tried to be all three, and that is what I try to teach others.

When we travel, we ask God for His grace to get us, our friends and those we love to our destinations safely. I asked God for His traveling grace in my life, and I believe that He has given me just that.

I thank you Jesus, for blessing me with Your traveling grace that has allowed me to shine. Amen.

Rev. Helene Walker is the founding Pastor of Realistic Ministries Inc. She is a writer, published author, and UAW Chaplain. She has a bachelor's degree in religious studies from Heritage College and Seminary in Ontario, Canada. She is married to Karlos and they have four adult children. They are also proud grandparents and great-grand parents. Her spiritual mission is to always be a person of integrity, to be obedient to God, to love people and to make disciples...as we are commissioned to do in Matthew 28:19-20. Her contact Information is: P.O. Box 970231, Ypsilanti, MI 48197, hsisterjay@aol.com

WHEN LIFE CREATES THE PERFECT STORM

Rev. Joyce Irvin Harris, M.Div.

My Father is rich in houses and lands,
He holdeth the wealth of the world in the palm of His Hands!
I am so glad
I am a child of the most high King.
Of rubies and diamonds, of silver and gold,
His coffers are full, He has so many riches untold.
I am so glad
I am a child of the most high King.
--James Cleveland, "Child of the King"

How many times have I sung that song with gusto in my heart and financial worry on my mind? I sang that song when I was poor in pocket, but rich in spirit. I told myself this was far more favorable than the reverse, because it's what a true child of God is expected to say. After all, God will make it alright eventually, in some distant future or on the other side. But what sense did it make to inherit God's riches when I got to heaven? I won't need riches when I get to heaven; I need riches on earth right now! The song didn't make sense, but I kept on singing, and wondering, and worrying, as did most of the working-class people in my church who were employed but half-past broke. Yet, I read about Abraham, Isaac, Job, David, and others whom God made rich. But I kept singing...

While on others Thou art calling, Do not pass me by.

--Fannie Crosby, "Pass Me Not, O Gentle Savior"

Fast forward to age forty-something. At this stage of my life, I'm preaching and teaching, singing and praying...and I'm still struggling. I'm sure I'm hearing God, but my life's a roller coaster, up and down. I never seem to reach my full potential in any area. I'm a reasonably intelligent person, so why am I not succeeding? I'm a Spirit-filled, tongue-talking believer. My life is not supposed to be like this. Something is wrong. I'm ministering to people who are getting saved. People are being filled with the Holy Spirit, yet I'm still unfulfilled and making life-sabotaging decisions. Little did I know that someone else's poor judgment would soon send me on a life-changing odyssey.

Sunday afternoon, August 23, 1998, started out as a beautiful day. In my pastor's absence, I preached the morning message and God blessed mightily. The glory of His *Shekinah* presence shone brightly. People got saved. People got filled with the Holy Spirit. Heaven was happy! Suddenly, while driving from church, I was hit by a drunken driver. I was hit so hard I saw colors! I tried to get out of the car, but never made it. God sent two ladies and a gentleman to assist me. The gentleman, a deacon in his church, was a Vietnam medic and an amputee. His banging on my car window roused me to consciousness. As I came around, I realized that my head and back were killing me! This wonderful gentleman stabilized me while one lady directed traffic and the other called my husband. After an ambulance ride and a few hours in the emergency room, I was sent home with my leg in a twenty-four-inch elastic universal knee immobilizer. My presenting injuries were categorized as "sprains and strains."

In the weeks that followed, I refused to be slowed down. I ministered, gave speeches, and did consulting work...though I bumped into walls, burned myself while cooking, and saw things crawling that no one else did. I hurt badly, had bouts with sleeplessness, felt crazy, confused, and suicidal. Yet to everyone, including my husband, I looked fine. Nonetheless, I sensed I was in more trouble than I'd ever experienced. And I was right.

About 9 weeks post-accident, I began showing subtle but more serious symptoms. Misuse of words was seen as a slip of the tongue. Forgetfulness was attributed to being overextended. Losing track of a thought, or "spacing out" in the middle of a conversation, was thought to be preoccupation. To everyone, I was still my normal self.

But "normal" I was not. It took great effort to be articulate. I couldn't focus on one task, so juggling several was not an option. I couldn't remember a thought long enough to complete a sentence. All this came to a humiliating head in the pulpit when I embarrassingly discovered, at a significant preaching engagement, that I could not preach—with or without a manuscript—because I couldn't follow the print on the page or accurately quote well-known Scriptures.

I felt people were whispering: "Whatever she had before, she definitely doesn't have it now!"

On another occasion, I discovered that I could not pray the pastoral prayer at altar call. The cacophony of sounds swirling around me was overwhelming. The congregation and the instruments overpowered my ability to hang on to a train of thought. I felt severely judged and people no longer beat a path to the front of the church to greet me. Those who found themselves in my path smiled politely and expressed perfunctory greetings. The whispering and murmuring was devastating: "She's lost the Anointing." I had lost something all right, but it wasn't the Anointing. I had lost much needed visual and cognitive abilities. Little did I know that all my difficulties would help me find answers about myself that I had spent a lifetime searching for.

Since even the people in whom I confided trivialized my condition, I could not risk permanently destroying the integrity of my ministry. Not knowing when or if I'd ever be able to return, I stepped down from the pulpit. It was one of the most emotionally painful decisions I ever made.

In addition to emotional pain, I battled intense and unrelenting physical pain...so severe that I had serious thoughts of suicide. Life had created the perfect storm and I couldn't see my way out. I couldn't read the Word. I couldn't recall the Word. I couldn't pray. I felt strongly that going home to Jesus was better than what I was experiencing. My short-term memory was nearly nonexistent. It took me seven times going in and out of the refrigerator to complete making a simple sandwich. Going grocery shopping meant that I'd be in the store for four hours and end up being found by a sympathetic employee...in tears, in pain, and confused...because even with a list, I was overwhelmed by all the choices. Because I was trying to juggle so many things, fatigue became my constant companion. The pain got so intense that I was finally forced to seek medical help. When I did, the "strains and sprains" diagnosis from the emergency room gave way to the more serious diagnosis of mild traumatic brain injury (MTBI), fibromyalgia, and myofascial pain. And the psychologist's "by the way" comment was, "Of course, you already know that you have Attention Deficit Hyperactivity Disorder (or ADHD)." Boom! I'm now truly engulfed in a perfect storm. After that diagnosis, I laughed and cried.

"Thank you, Jesus! At last! Confirmation! I don't have a character flaw wherein I lack commitment or the willpower to see a task through. I have a chemical deficiency in the management system of my brain!"

The craziness I experienced from childhood that seemed to hijack my fulfillment finally had a name. The irritability and bluntness that made me seem like the stereotypical "angry black woman" was finally identified. The disorganization and lack of time consciousness that frustrated and embarrassed me was rooted in an identifiable cause—ADHD. Finally, a diagnosis! Sigh! Who knew? Now I have a traumatic brain injury on top of a long-standing brain disorder.

Satan, have you tried My servant, Joyce?

Once diagnosed, therapy consumed me. The Holy Spirit led me to the most phenomenal medical team of brain injury specialists to be found! I had a neuropsychologist, psychiatrist, neuro-optometrist, physiatrist, chiropractor, physical rehabilitation therapist, and others. They provided me with psychotherapy, eye therapy, pain therapy, chiropractic adjustments, craniosacral massage therapy, vocational therapy, occupational therapy, physical therapy, acupuncture, and a support group. I made phenomenal strides in my recovery, but there were still some things that were missing. Some things were broken and were not expected to get better. Though none of my injuries were physically life-threatening, I still felt like I was "walking through the valley of the shadow of death." Sadly, my husband could not go through the valley with me and my marriage ended. I was now not only grieving the loss of self, but also the loss of my marriage. This is when my journey into a deeper faith began. The invisible brain injury and all the "stuff" that went with it were the straws that irreparably broke my already floundering marriage. My husband did not believe that I was as injured as I and my neuropsychologist said. He could not understand that I had energy for some things but not for others. Because I am also a clinician, my husband felt that my psychologist and I were in collusion and would tell him anything I wanted. I was hurt by my husband, because he wouldn't fight for our marriage. I was wounded, because he wanted out even though I was very ill.

I needed to express my anger. Through all of my sessions to that point, I had been totally rational. But you don't come through that kind of injury, pain, and loss without being angry. Yet, I could not identify with whom I was angry. One of my therapists felt I should have been angry with the driver who hit me and fled on foot without so much as a call for help. My irritation with him was short-lived. I was angry with him for totaling my car and ruining my Sunday afternoon. He was inebriated and stupid and not worth more consideration than I'd already given him.

During one tense meeting, my therapist asked, "Where was your God when this drunk hit you and left without calling for help?"

All I could think of was how God had sent those women and the Vietnam medic to help me. By now, I'm upset and pacing to and fro.

I told my therapist: "The enemy comes to steal, kill, and destroy; but God said, 'Not so!' The Adversary prowls to and fro in the earth as a roaring lion, seeking who he may devour. What the enemy meant for evil..."

What the enemy meant for evil...

As I speak, I'm pacing faster and speaking louder and more emphatically.

"The enemy has robbed me of my transportation, my ability to work, my physical health, my sanity, my cognition, and my memory. Let him who stole, steal no more! ENOUGH!"

I began to speak in tongues because I found tongues bypassed my MTBI. I was angry with Satan and on a righteous rant, speaking God's truth to the Evil One. I slipped fluidly between my spiritual and earthly languages as if I were interpreting myself. Each time I spoke with understanding in my natural tongue, the interpretation came from the Scriptures.

"You came to steal, kill, and destroy; but Jesus came to give me abundant life here and now. You should have killed me while you had the chance, devil, because greater is God who is in me than you who are in this world. I can do all things through Christ Who strengthens me. I will get better because He was wounded for my transgressions, bruised for my iniquities...the chastisement for my peace was put on Him, and BY HIS STRIPES I AM HEALED!"

I finally came to myself and looked around. My therapist was looking at me uneasily.

I snapped at him: "You're Jewish! He was YOUR Holy Ghost before He was mine!"

The therapist wrote in his notes that I had experienced a "hysterical episode."

The clinical director, who was also my primary therapist, came in and said, "I hear we've achieved breakthrough!"

I was adamant that any reference to hysterics be removed from my record. I explained that I went from anger to warfare praying. I explained that praying in tongues is a spiritual tactic that unleashes the power of God's Word as an offensive weapon. I was exhausted when I left that therapy session, but I sang this Pentecostal war cry all the way home.

I'm a soldier (in the Army of the Lord
Got my war clothes on (in the Army)
Got my sword and shield (in the Army of the Lord)
I'm a sanctified soldier (in the Army)

What the enemy meant for evil, God turned into the most spiritually productive time of my life! The teachings from my youth laid a foundation. I was Biblically literate, but clueless on how to consistently apply the power and authority that God has given His people for all aspects of our lives. I knew God had a specific plan for me. I had fulfilled part of God's plan, but did not know how to position myself to bring His full plan into fruition. God used my spiritual time-out for recovery and rehabilitation and to spiritually "retool and re-school" me. He led me on an "educational sabbatical" away from my familiar (and comfortable) denominational tradition to attend a nondenominational church with emphasis on applying Biblical principles and power to daily life. Finally, the missing piece!

My ministerial sabbatical lasted 8 years. In the interim, my vision healed, my brain retrained itself and my cognitive abilities improved. I am not the person I was prior to the accident. That person no longer exists. However, I learned how to maximize the cognitive functions that remain. While healing, I worked with a partner to design and deliver cultural competence training for the El Paso County, Colorado juvenile justice system. I did organizational culture consulting with a few Fortune 500 companies. I facilitated a few retreats.

And I became an affiliate faculty member for a Jesuit university where I taught undergraduate psychology, sociology, and religious studies for fifteen years. The perfect storm that hit me was fierce. When it ended, it left a high functioning brain injury survivor in its wake who successfully lives with challenges that most people don't recognize. One such major challenge was the mild stroke I had in 2008. I am fortunate that I incurred no paralysis; it just scrambled my cognition even more. Words are my life. Yet they escape me to places unknown on a regular basis. Still, through it all, the "Son" shines even brighter through the person I am now. I returned to active ministry ablaze with Holy Ghost fire. I have a message of empowerment that totally aligns with the call He gave me many years ago.

Oh, how I praise God for my journey! August 2017 marks nineteen years since my accident. The knowledge I've gained of the God-consciousness within is enabling me to reposition myself so that, as God promised, my latter years will indeed be greater than my past.

Reverend Joyce Irvin Harris, M.Div., is the Associate Minister of Christian Education at the Historic Little Rock Baptist Church of Detroit and is a graduate of the University of Detroit and Morehouse School of Religion at the Interdenominational Theological Center in Atlanta, Georgia. Upon completion of seminary, she was the first woman ordained by the late civil rights leader, Reverend Dr. Ralph David Abernathy and the West Hunter Street Baptist Church. Reverend Harris has provided pastoral leadership to civilian congregations and, as a Navy chaplain, to military personnel and families in sea service commands ashore and afloat. She can be reached by email at: wjiharris@yahoo.com.

CAN I NOT DO WITH YOU?

Rev. Doris B. Ryans

As I look back, I now am able to see that my life has been a process of preparation toward fulfilling my life's purpose, which is ministering to women. I was raised in a Christian home with parents who attended church service twice weekly, as well as Sunday school. They were also active on the Usher Board and sang in the choir. As far back as I can remember, praying, singing church hymns, and reading the Bible were a part of my life. As I matured physically, I also matured spiritually.

Entering adulthood, I faced many challenging situations: marriage at the age of 20, childbirth, the death of my sister, and divorce. Life wasn't easy and over time, bitterness and anger consumed me, and I became dissatisfied with life and the hand it had seemingly dealt me. Before I married, I had an idealistic view of what married life would be like. What started out as marital bliss soon changed as challenges arose. Adding a new baby to our household, combined with periods of unemployment, led to financial strain. Also, from the start, our marriage did not have the proper foundation. You see, shortly after our wedding, I found out that my husband had joined the church only so I could have my church wedding. This was an outward action that did not involve an inward change to his heart. Thus, I found myself unequally yoked. The infidelity of, and subsequent decision by, my husband that married life was not for him left me a single mother with a toddler. I was a woman with damaged self-esteem...questioning my desirability.

While going through my divorce, I lost my baby sister, Brenda, on July 1, 1983...a day forever etched in my heart. I received a call that morning from my mother telling me to get to the hospital as quickly as I could because Brenda had taken a turn for the worse. I was in disbelief, because the previous night I had sat on her hospital bed, brushing her hair as we talked excitedly about her coming home for the 4th of July holiday. I remember that it rained that night...a real downpour that flooded the streets as I made my way from the north side of Detroit to Ecorse. Little did I know that, after that night, my life would never be the same. As I stood outside the doors of the ICU waiting for the surgical team to wheel my sister into surgery, I heard the words "Code Blue." I watched as the surgical team, my sister's only hope for survival, walked solemnly out. I recall that a sharp piercing pain struck my heart as I stood there. Shortly thereafter, someone came to escort our family to a waiting room. They confirmed what I had felt in my heart, that my little sister was gone.

With my self-esteem already damaged, I struggled with thoughts that maybe it should have been me who died. In desperate times, the enemy can take your thoughts captive before he attacks you at the place of your greatest weakness. For years, my weakness had always been my low self-esteem. Of the two of us, I was the fair-skinned, chubby one. I was the one who struggled to get B's in school. I was the strong-willed one who was always stretching the rules. I was the one who couldn't make my marriage work...the one who had walked away angry at God. The way things were going in my life, surely my dying would just be another fatality in a life that seemed to have no meaning anyway.

After my sister's death, I appeared to be holding things together...on the outside. However, on the inside, I was broken. At the age of twenty-six, my world had turned upside down! My life spiraled into darkness for two years. My attendance at church became sporadic because I blamed God for my sister's death! In my grief, I had trouble understanding how God could let my sister—someone who loved Him so—someone who was so gifted and so committed to serving the church, die at such a young age. In my anger, I felt that if God was this unloving, why did I need Him in my life?

I tried to relieve my pain by going from relationship to relationship. I also indulged in foolish spending. After suffering the infidelity of my spouse, I felt very unlovable and rejected. I sought validation and self-worth in relationships that only provided temporary satisfaction...and that resulted in feelings of shame. Believing it didn't matter if I lived a long life, I lived each day as if it were my last. In the past, I used to greet each day with joy and excitement. However, after my divorce and my sister's death, I suffered from bouts of depression and feelings of unworthiness. This was not the life I had envisioned, but it seemed like circumstances beyond my control were charting the course of my life. I even questioned if God had made a mistake by taking my sister and not me. Though I knew I wasn't living the life God wanted for me, I felt unable to break the negative cycle in my life. But, thanks be to God, the darkness that permeated my soul and my heart didn't signal the end my story.

A pivotal point in my life occurred when one of my girlfriends invited me to attend a Christian Women's Retreat in Traverse City. That Saturday, I listened as an anointed woman of God shared her life story. She had also experienced a failed marriage. She too had been rejected by her husband because she could not bear children. Soon, she was filled with bitterness and anger that consumed her life. I listened as she shared how God ministered to her when she visited a pottery factory during a trip to Amsterdam. She said she watched how the potter molded and shaped the clay in his hands until it became the image the potter had in mind. If the clay didn't conform itself to what the potter had in mind, he didn't throw the clay away. He just continued to mold and shape the clay until it became what he desired...a beautiful piece of art. The speaker shared that, as she stood there watching the potter, the Lord showed her that this process was an analogy of what God wanted to do in her life.

Though I was sitting in a room with over 500 women, the more the speaker spoke, the more the crowd seemed to dwindle from my perception. After a time, everything faded until I felt as if I were sitting alone in that big room.

In the quietness, I heard a still small voice speak to me: "Can I not do with you Doris? Can I not do with you?"

I felt my heart unlock as the Lord showed me that He wasn't through with me yet.

In my spirit, I replied, "Yes" to God's peaceful voice.

As battered and shattered as I was, I knew in my heart that God could fix my brokenness. I knew that He would mold and shape me into a work of art. At that moment, a transformation came over me. I felt it first in my heart and then in my mind as I allowed God's love to fill me. That was the moment I decided to shine!

I left that conference having recommitted my life to God. Everything that had been shattered and broken in me began to heal. I realized that God had a unique purpose for my life, and my imperfections did not matter. In fact, each scar, each blemish, and each crack became part of my life's story. All I had to do was let God do with my life what that potter did to his pottery: mold me in His loving hands. No longer would I live with no thought of tomorrow. No longer would I live a lifestyle that did not glorify God. No longer would I allow negative situations in my life to enshroud me. Instead, I would honor my sister's memory by living a life that exemplified the Godly virtues she embodied.

I began to immerse myself in God's Word. I created affirmations from scripture that I read daily, as they affirmed who I was in Christ. My self-image began to heal as I allowed His Word to become my truth. My hope in a promising future was restored as I meditated upon Jeremiah 29:11: *"For I know the thoughts that I think toward you, says the Lord, thoughts of peace and not of evil, to give you a future and a hope."* (NKJV)

My self-esteem was restored as I realized that Someone greater than man found me to be desirable and worthy, as John 15:16 states: *"Ye have not chosen me, but I have chosen you...that whatsoever ye shall ask of the Father in my name, he may give it you." (KJV)* My feelings of shame evaporated as I began to believe the words in *Isaiah 1:18: "...though your sins be as scarlet, they shall be as white as snow."*

God had forgiven me, but now I had to forgive myself. I had done so many wrong things when I strayed from God...things that didn't glorify Him. Meditating on and speaking these scriptures became my mantra. Day by day, I saw a shift occur in my life as my relationship with God was restored. Once I reaffirmed that I was created, chosen, and loved by God, I no longer felt worthless. As I grew in grace, my insecurities as a woman, my low self-esteem, and my need for validation from others began to diminish. This process didn't occur overnight. There were still times of feeling as though I was unworthy. But when those feelings arose, I would determine that my past would not overshadow my future.

As my relationship with God deepened, I had a growing desire to study and teach God's Word. I began to serve the Lord by sharing the spiritual gifts He gave me. I became active in Christian education. I started teaching Sunday School and Bible Study. I began to speak at various church functions: prayer breakfasts, Women's Day celebrations, workshops, etc. God began to show me there was a purpose for all I had been through. He showed me that there was a *message* to be found in my *mess* and a *testimony* to be birthed out of my *tests.* Everything that I had endured prepared me to minister to women in situations where they also feel broken and unlovable. If you are one of these women, I want you to know that God has a plan and a purpose for your life. Contrary to what others may have spoken about you, you are redeemable and can be healed and restored. In fact, my healing led me to establish Divinely Blessed & Restored Ministry as my passion and call to preach and teach God's Word burned deeper and stronger within me.

I began to earnestly seek direction from God and the counsel of my pastor, the late Joseph B. Barlow, Jr. At times, I struggled with the notion that God could really use me. After all, I was the one who had walked away from a relationship with Him. I was the one with the scarlet past who struggled with low self-esteem. How could such a one as I hold the office of preacher and teacher? I needed answers. Because I am a person who approaches life very cautiously and with great deliberation, I needed God to reveal His answer to me in a manner that was tailor-made for my personality and nature.

One Sunday, while seated in church, God affirmed my call in a vision. As I looked upon the pulpit, it was transformed in my vision. I saw myself standing there preaching. In this vision I heard the words I'd heard several years previously at the conference in Traverse City: "Can I not do with you, Doris? Can I not do with you?" At that moment, I knew beyond a shadow of a doubt that I was called to proclaim the Gospel! I accepted His call and preached my trial sermon on January 11, 2008, and was ordained as a minister on November 7, 2008.

As I write this, my life has been totally transformed. I wake each morning excited at the prospect of what God has in store! I no longer hide the truths of my past. I freely reveal the circumstances of my journey. I joyfully minister about how God's power can move a person from darkness into His light. I am determined that I will not let the fear of other people's perception of me silence me or shame me back into a life of hiding. My decision to live authentically has allowed me to shine with greater brilliance. With clarity of purpose, I am excited to be a vessel through which God's spoken word repairs cracks, removes blemishes, and brings healing to God's daughters. I rejoice when I see a woman accept her true identity as a Daughter of the King! It is my desire that every woman, every girl will walk in the light. I pray that you find the same realization that I found...that you are precious in God's sight. Once you realize this in your heart, this truth will manifest itself in your life.

No matter your story, it can be rewritten if you allow yourself to be molded by the Master. If your life seems murky, I encourage you to embrace the truth of who you are and "whose" you are. When you operate in your truth, your life will be set upon a sure foundation and your healing journey can begin. Your healing starts with an honest evaluation of your life. Speaking your truth will lead to a transformation of your body, soul and mind. Renew your mind and submit yourself to the Master, allowing Him to mold and shape you for the life He predestined for you. Once you do this, you too will shine.

Stop listening to the worldly standards that declare you are "less than." Pledge each day to live authentically, no longer hiding your truth. Let your truth empower and propel your life. If someone attempts to define your future by your past, remember that you are redeemed and delivered from your past. With gratitude, thank God for your life's journey and the paths you have traveled. Every step forward in your journey will lead you to freedom from guilt and shame. Be free! Let no one or no-thing (nothing) dim or extinguish your light! See yourself as God sees you. Believe that you are a precious piece of art...designed and defined by God. Believe that you have a unique purpose to fulfill. When you have done these things, you too can answer God's question: "Can I not do with you?" with a resounding "Yes, Lord, do with me as You will!" When you speak your truth to power, you will also shine!

Rev. Doris B. Ryans is a Spirit-filled, sought after preacher and teacher. She is the mother of one daughter, Kristyn (David) and two grandsons, Suruli and Donald Joshua, who are the apples of her eye. An Ordained Minister at Mt. Zion Missionary Baptist Church, under the leadership of Pastor Kevin B. Mack, she provides leadership to the Women's Ministry. She proclaims healing and restoration to the broken through Divinely Blessed & Restored Ministry, which was organized in 2005. Retired after twenty-five years of administrative court service, she is currently employed as a manager at Marygrove College. Rev. Ryans can be reached via email at dbrministry2007@gmail.com or (313) 308-6310.

TEACH ME TO SHINE

Linda Thornton M.A. NCC/LPC, ACS

As I write this chapter, my thoughts go far back in time to when I was a very young child...growing up in a family with my Mom and seven siblings. I was the youngest in the group; the next child was eleven years older than I. At times, I wished that I had been born a twin so I could have had a sister or a brother my age as a companion. My siblings' father died several years before I was born. My mother and father separated when I was very young. Even though my biological father wasn't always active in my life, I had older brothers and uncles who filled the void. I remember my Dad picking me up on occasion and taking me over to his mother's home, my Grandmother's house, where I would spend weekends. Those times were so enjoyable...and some Sundays she would take me with her to church. I remember one Sunday attending church with my Grandma. The church was sponsoring a fundraiser and the person who raised the most money received special recognition and a prize. Well, my Grandma made sure that I raised the most funds and I received the prize. I remember how great I felt that Sunday. She always gave me gifts to bring home when I visited her. My Grandma was someone to be adored. She lived a long life and one of my aunts said that Grandma was 102 years old when she died.

When I was around the age of five or six, I remember losing a brother in the Korean Conflict and seeing my mother buckle to her knees when the soldiers came to tell her that he was missing in action. Shortly after that, the military confirmed that my brother had been killed during the war. Our family was advised to leave his casket closed at the funeral. Not being able to view his body left uncertainties in our minds. I was too young to really express my grief at that time or to even know what I was feeling. I watched everyone else as they mourned. To compound this loss, my mother died when I was twelve years old. I had the same sense of loss when she died, but by this age, I had a better understanding of grief. I felt the pain that comes with losing someone you deeply loved. Her death brought about major changes in my life and her transition meant that I had to immediately take on more responsibilities. It was as though I became a young adult at the age of twelve.

It's hard to put into words how I felt about my departed family members. It was not until I was in my late twenties that I was able to fully grieve my brother's and my mother's deaths and get past their loss. By this time, I was married and had two wonderful children. But after thirteen years of marriage, I ended up in a divorce. Looking back, there were red flags throughout those thirteen years that signaled my marriage was in deep trouble.

In hindsight, I learned many lessons from my failed marriage. One important nugget of wisdom that I learned is that a married couple must be real and truthful with one another and work together as one. They must genuinely accept each other as a total, complete person.

A mental health therapist, Dr. Albert Ellis (1994) describes it this way, "Accept each other as is."

Oftentimes our focus and expectations are on what we think our spouse could be or should do, rarely accepting him or her totally for who he or she is now. Couples must accept themselves individually and acknowledge their faults, shortcomings, feelings, and thoughts. And, last but not least, as an intricate and pertinent part of my learning process, I learned that couples must know God and have a relationship with Him. A marriage burdened by pretense is sure to fail. I am remarried to a wonderful, Godly man and I thank God for His radiance in our lives. I am using the valuable lessons that I learned early on to help me in my current marriage. I also use these principles in my ministry when assisting couples who are experiencing marital and relationship difficulties.

Today, as I think about all my past experiences...my successes as well as my failures...and what stands out the most is that God was involved throughout my life. He prepared me from childhood to serve Him and allow His light to radiate through me. He prepared me to encourage, teach and do all the work that He assigned me to do. I can easily recall certain incidents that happened in my childhood home that caused concern and worry. I was intuitively aware and observant of my brothers' and sisters' behavior and temperament, especially when they had heated arguments and sometimes physically fought one another. They didn't pay much attention to me during their quarrels because of my young age, but I really wanted to make peace. I didn't know exactly how to help them. I know now that this period in my life was a fertile training ground, where I learned by observation how family members interact and behave with each other during times of conflict and crisis.

As I grew into adulthood, I made mistakes of my own. At times, I struggled with guilt and shame and was sometimes my own worst enemy...while everyone else seemed to be living their lives with ease. But after struggling along in life, I had an awakening. I knew that I needed to restore my relationship with God and have Him become more active in my life. This was what I desperately needed in order to have the peace and joy that I desired—even as a child watching my brothers and sisters feud with each other. I'm thankful that a friend invited me to attend a skating outing that her church sponsored. I accepted her invitation and when I visited her church, I was warmly received. There was such a friendly feeling there that I went back again and again. I eventually became a member of the church, which was the best thing that I could have done at that time. After having no peace for so long, I repented and received God's provision and forgiveness for my sins. Under the tutelage and spiritual guidance of the Pastor, I learned God's ways. I learned how He deals with people in conflict...through compassion and grace. He makes these things readily available to all who submit to Him. Through my life experiences, I have come to know God in a special way. I learned His attributes and how He deals with broken people. After receiving God's mercy and grace, I know now that He was directing and orchestrating the course of my life all the while. He was with me even as I was growing up without my father's presence in our home.

God has given me a heart of compassion to assist people who are experiencing the same challenges, losses and difficulties in their lives that I experienced. He also taught me to share His love with those who have not yet come into the knowledge, understanding, and acceptance of Him as their Lord. Because God transformed my life, I am passionate about seeing people strengthened and restored through counseling and teaching His Word...helping them build personal relationships with Him. I believe that people become whole spiritually, mentally, physically, and socially when they are connected to their Source. Individuals and families are restored as their relationship with God grows. And people will help one another and carry out God's great commandment to love one another when they experience the love that He has for us.

Although I made mistakes and was undisciplined in some areas of my life, God was always merciful and compassionate towards me. He made it possible for me to work jobs or attend schools and workshops that prepared me for the counseling profession that I'm in today. He would direct my path to connect with other people who had like-minded passions. Some of the people I met added great value to my life by providing direction and training...or encouraging me to set goals and achieve them. At other times, I needed to be challenged; and God made that happen when necessary. My first job after moving to Michigan was working with mentally and physically challenged people who lived in a state-run institution. I think God was building and shaping my character through this job. I was responsible for the total care of bedridden, dependent patients in the infirmary. I enjoyed my job, and later earned a promotion from attendant nurse to supervisor.

After my promotion, I accepted a job in a regional center, working with moderately mentally challenged (but ambulatory) residents who led active lives. My job was to supervise and train staff, participate with an interdisciplinary team for the care and welfare of the residents, meet with their relatives/guardians, and oversee and manage day to day operations of the units assigned to me. Even though this was not a faith-based institution, God taught me a lot about leadership and administration and how to work, not only with the residents, but also with the staff. He also taught me how to let His light shine through me as He sharpened the gifts He placed within me. I also sought higher education while working full-time with The State of Michigan. Because of

God's prompting and guidance, one of my supervisors at the Department of Mental Health told me about a program in gerontology at a nearby university not far from where I worked. I sent my application in and was accepted into the program. I earned a B.S. degree in Gerontology while being a mom and working a full-time job. I'm sharing this because you may be thinking of returning to school or achieving your dreams. Don't allow negative thoughts or circumstances stop you from reaching your goals. Adversity and difficulty can be leveraged to propel you further ahead into achieving your dreams. What you believe, you can achieve.

Because of the desire God instilled in me to help others, I enrolled in a seminary where I earned a master's degree in counseling. I currently teach part-time at the graduate level in a Christian university where professors are encouraged to make God's presence known within the classroom setting. As an instructor, I'm passionate about seeing students become professional counselors through embodying Christ-like character and attributes.

On January 8, 2002, I founded TOUCH Services, LLC, a counseling agency. I currently provide individual and group counseling, and I truly enjoy my work.

Being raised by my mom and older siblings, as a child I did not have a clue what my future as an adult might be. Society would have written me off, but God knew the entire time all the wonderful things He had planned for me. When I suffered the early losses of my brother and mother, and two other siblings who died later, God was with me the entire time. When I was older and strayed away from His path, He stayed with me and never left me. He continues to fine-tune my life today and increase my desire for a closer relationship with Him. I am a member of Christian Tabernacle Church in

Southfield, Michigan, where I attend weekly services. I take classes at a Bible Institute so that I can be an effective witness in letting God's light shine through me. I also attend workshops and seminars to keep current with trends in counseling. On occasion, I facilitate seminars and workshops. In the past, I felt intimidated and inadequate when standing before people and speaking, but now my confidence comes from God. During the past eight years, He has blessed my private practice to sponsor annual ladies' spring luncheons...encouraging, refreshing and building women up in their faith so that they can live wholesome, fulfilled, Godly lives.

I cannot talk about letting my light shine without giving God praise for His blessings upon my life. Through the ups-and-downs of my life, God has given me His peace, a loving husband, wonderful children, loving grandchildren, great-grandchildren and a host of supportive relatives and friends. I have come to know Him as a loving Father who provides all my needs. I also desire these things for my family and for those whom I teach, serve, and counsel at my private practice. I believe that a life well lived is one that has God at its core. The same wisdom that was given to the early Church applies to us today. That is, having Jesus Christ as the Chief Cornerstone of our faith. (Eph. 2:19-21) If we are connected to God (John 15:5) and obey His commands, we will live prosperous lives and our light will shine brightly. (Jeremiah 29:11)

God continues to reveal new realities to me day by day. I'm thankful to Him for making me whole and bringing me this far, giving me a heart of empathy and compassion for people who are broken.

Writing this chapter motivated me to reflect over my life and actually see God's hand of correction, grace, mercy, love, and blessing along my path. He never, ever left me alone...and I am eternally grateful to Him for giving me life.

Linda Thornton is a Licensed Professional Counselor and Founder of TOUCH Services, LLC. She is also an adjunct faculty member at Spring Arbor University. Linda earned an MA in Counseling and a B.S. in Gerontology. She is certified as an Approved Clinical Supervisor and a National Certified Counselor. She was awarded the Ned Adams, Jr. Counseling Award by Ashland Theological Seminary. Linda's passion is helping clients overcome challenges to achieve their goals. She holds workshops and luncheons through her private practice. Linda joined Christian Tabernacle Church in Southfield, Michigan, under the leadership of Dr. James and Mrs. Loretta Morman. Before retiring, Linda worked for the State of Michigan for thirty-three years. Linda and her husband Charles share a wonderfully blended family of four children and several grandchildren and great-grandchildren. Linda can be contacted by phone at (313) 537-7230 or through: https://therapists.psychologytoday.com

SHINE SPECIAL FEATURE: I'M A SURVIVOR

Dr. Eunice Mosley Dudley
Humanitarian and Entrepreneur

In June 2017, Dr. Eunice Mosley Dudley, along with her family and several other distinguished entrepreneurs, celebrated her ex-husband Joe L. Dudley Sr.'s eightieth birthday. Along with Mr. Dudley, the gala, held in Winston-Salem, North Carolina, also feted Mr. S. B. Fuller and other African-American business leaders. The affair was also an occasion to support fundraising efforts for an Entrepreneurship Museum in honor of pioneers of the black business community. The celebration's theme was "Capitalism: The Only True Pathway To Freedom."

A pioneer herself, Dr. Dudley co-founded the Dudley Q+ brand, along with husband Joe L. Dudley, nearly fifty years ago. The Dudley hair care empire includes cosmetology schools and beauty products. A highly respected and sought-after business mogul, Dr. Dudley currently serves as Executive Director of the Dudley Beauty School System. Throughout her tenure at the company, she has worked in nearly every area of the business: sales, manufacturing, administration, etc. Additionally, she is a respected humanitarian who believes in giving back to the community.

She is also a cancer survivor, having been diagnosed sixteen years ago with a rare form of histoid breast carcinoma. When we met with her in June 2017, we extended an invitation to share her story in our anthology, Shine: Hidden No Longer: Sisters Light Up the World Through Speaking Truth to Power, and she graciously agreed.

As is her custom, she related her remarkable story in her always sociable and elegant way.

A Difficult Diagnosis

When Dr. Dudley was diagnosed, it was a complete shock and left her stunned, because she always had regularly scheduled mammograms. In addition, her case was difficult because there was no treatment for her particular form of cancer. At the time, only one article had been written about histoid carcinoma in thirty-six years.

"My daughters were with me in the doctor's office," she remembers. "When they heard me say that I wanted to proceed with the recommended treatments they said, 'Mama, don't you want to wait and get a second opinion?'"

Her daughters wanted her to wait a couple of weeks and find a specialist who might have given her a different diagnosis. However, Dr. Dudley bravely faced her situation and told them she didn't want to waste any time.

I told my daughters, "I've seen the biopsy results. When the medical team showed me what the scans looked like, I didn't need to be convinced of what I saw."

She reflects: "I already knew what I had to do. I knew I needed to get rid of this thing instead of letting it grow faster and bigger. I told my girls, 'Let's do what we have to do to get it taken care of. I don't want to be running around trying to get a second opinion.' That was the only time that I had anyone speaking contrary to my thoughts. After that, they knew to leave Mama alone."

Pressing Past Fear

After Dr. Dudley received her diagnosis and made a firm commitment to undergo treatment, she reacted with strength under fire as she set her mind to overcome this daunting challenge.

"I did not fall apart. There were no tears and I did not whimper! I didn't feel sorry for myself. Because I deal in positivity all of the time, I wasn't going to let this diagnosis shatter me or throw me off of what I was doing."

True to her word, she did not allow her breast cancer diagnosis to extinguish her passion for living. She faced her circumstances head on and without apology. Courageously, she decided to announce her cancer diagnosis at the Dudley Educational and Motivational Symposium hair show. She boldly shared with the fourteen-hundred attendees that she had already had surgery and that she would be starting chemotherapy. She decided to go public with the announcement for several reasons.

"Cosmetologists, barbers and others who work in the beauty industry deal with clients who lose their hair all the time. Whether the hair loss is because of genetic or medical reasons, many of these clients feel ashamed or awkward. They don't want people to know."

Dr. Dudley wanted people to talk about their hair loss, no matter the cause. She also wanted to talk about cancer, because she sees it as being no different than any other ailment or health issue. One of her philosophies is that you can save your life if you talk openly about your diagnosis.

Dr. Dudley is passionate about people speaking their truth openly: "I want people to know what to expect. Many people don't know the difference between chemotherapy and radiation. When I have speaking opportunities, I talk about cancer so that people know that it can be treated."

She is a firm believer in getting help as early in the treatment process as possible.

"I know for myself that cancer can be treated early if diagnosed early," she states emphatically. "I know that a cancer diagnosis can be devastating if you don't catch it until the last stage of the disease. If you don't get treatment right away, the doctors have to fight so much harder to save your life."

She strongly believes that an educated patient is their own best advocate. She also stresses that patients need to stay positive during their process.

"The more you understand, the better you can deal with your healing process. I concentrated on total positivity during my treatment. I didn't allow negativity or people around me crying. I refused to deal with strange or pitying looks and I refused to worry about other peoples' opinions."

After receiving her diagnosis and a variety of options for treatment, Dr. Dudley chose a course of treatment that included chemotherapy, lumpectomy surgery of her breast and radiation therapy. Her doctors estimated that this three-pronged process would provide an eighty-five percent chance for her healing.

"I wanted to live a long life so I chose all three options," she said.

Cancer treatments can be very hard on a patient's body. In some cases, the side effects can be debilitating and energy draining. Dr. Dudley experienced some of these side effects.

"Chemotherapy can be rough on your body, particularly your skin and hair. It can even cause numbness of your toes and feet. As many people know, chemotherapy can make your hair fall out."

The irony of her being a beauty mogul whose hair could fall out wasn't lost on Dr. Dudley. However, her lifelong experience in the beauty business and knowing her craft so well was a plus for her. She refused to let the thought of losing her hair upset her.

"When I thought of what I'd do if my hair fell out, I didn't panic," she remembers with a smile. "I figured that if I couldn't grow my hair back, it would be okay. After all, I am in the hair business. I know people who can put a weave in, style a wig, or put hair onto a bald scalp."

Amazingly, Dr. Dudley kept up her strenuous work schedule despite the rigors of her therapy. She scheduled radiation therapy at the end of her workday so that she didn't have to worry about going back to work. She also found creative ways to deal with the difficulties that her treatment presented.

"Radiation treatment can burn the flesh," she said thoughtfully. "I met a lady who didn't seem to be burned and asked her what she did to keep her skin from getting dark. She explained that she lightly dusted the target area on her breast with corn starch. That sounded good to me, so I asked my primary care nurse if I could do the same thing and she said, "Yes." So, I got a bag of corn starch and a cosmetic brush and dusted the targeted area on my breast."

Because Dr. Dudley opted for radiation as part of her treatment plan, she had to have special equipment to make sure that the only area on her body that was radiated was the affected spot on her breast.

"Because radiation therapy is so intensive, a cast mold was created so that each time I was treated my body was in the same position. I had to wear that mold every time I had radiation. It took longer to get placed in the mold than to undergo the actual treatment."

Throughout all her treatment, Dr. Dudley kept her spirits up and lifted up those around her, keeping them informed and updated on her progress on a regular basis.

"You don't have to be sad or down while undergoing cancer treatment," she firmly stated. "Look for the good in all of it."

Dr. Dudley never backed down from openly discussing her cancer battle with those who needed to hear it. She also gained deeper compassion for what other cancer patients went through during their own treatment process.

"A cancer patient needs to have compassion more than sympathy," she stated. "I encourage people who know someone undergoing treatment to offer them compassion that uplifts them."

She also recognizes that, though everyone undergoes different treatments, many also have a need for privacy while in the treatment area.

"I found that men especially need privacy during their cancer treatments," she related. "I myself like beauty salon suites because they are more private for hair loss patients."

Dr. Dudley recognizes that some people find it very difficult to talk about their cancer diagnosis and some even describe it as the "C" word. However, because she was given educational materials after her diagnosis, she feels that they helped her to better understand and deal with her treatment process.

"The entire time that I received my treatments wasn't bad," she recalls. "Even before I had chemo or radiation therapy, I attended a class on what to expect."

Dr. Dudley recollects that she still has much of the educational material that was given to her before her treatment.

"I still have my personal journal; and I took a class that the Cancer Society offered called "Look Good and Feel Better." This class taught me what I needed to know about the disease, showed me how to prevent infection, and how to best take care of myself. As a result, I felt good about my treatment."

The Formula for Success

Dr. Dudley exudes great positivity and lives by it daily. Her outlook has helped her become the successful woman she is today. The seeds for her positive outlook, as well as her business acumen, were sown early in her life. She spent her summers in Brooklyn, New York, with her aunt, Francis McGhee, who recently passed away. It is through her aunt that she was connected with the Fuller Products Company.

"I started selling door-to-door for Fuller in 1960 and attended regular meetings on how to do door-to-door sales. Those meetings taught me to how to be positive, how to not get uptight, and how to give good customer service."

At the time, Dr. Dudley's branch manager and his wife belonged to Dr. Norman Vincent Peale's church. Dr. Peale, an author, minister, and founder of Guideposts magazine, was a champion of "the power of positive thinking." To this day, Dr. Peale's philosophy continues to inspire new generations with his legacy of inspiration and optimism. Dr. Dudley recalls being fortunate in experiencing Dr. Peale's beliefs up close and personal.

"Many Sundays, Joe and I would go to Dr. Peale's church service. His messages kept me positive; he was one of the most positive ministers that anyone could ever meet. Dr. Peale is one of the main reasons that I developed a positive mindset."

On Achieving Success

There is no doubt that Dr. Dudley is a highly successful businesswoman. She has remained one of the top female entrepreneurs for the past fifty years. When asked to share her wisdom about starting a business, she is very generous and enthusiastic. Her words can be used as a primer for success by any woman who wants to succeed in business. Her most important suggestion is for women to find a mentor.

"I am big on having a mentor. Having someone who has actually experienced what you may potentially go through is very important. Seek a mentor, so that you don't run into the same obstacles as others. Even if you're not in the same business as your mentor, you can still receive help."

Dr. Dudley also offers five key components for women who want to be entrepreneurs:

- Get rid of fear.
- Look for the niche that fits you.
- Be tenacious about finding help.
- Seek training and take classes.
- Contact your local Chamber of Commerce and use their knowledge to improve your business.

Final Words

Dr. Dudley says that women today are more aware of business opportunities and are taking advantage of them. She feels that women in her day were more frightened of stepping out. She is pleased to see more women moving up the corporate ladder and stretching out into many business markets. She believes that success is all about the individual. She believes that women need to determine how much they are willing to invest in themselves. Then they must plan and execute their ideas to the fullest.

"Women are being creative and opting to take advantage of opportunities," Dr. Dudley relates proudly. "Women know they can keep their corporate job and still be an entrepreneur on the side. More women are willing to step out."

Any story about Dr. Dudley would be incomplete without a very illuminating anecdote about how she stays at the top her field. In July 2015, the Greensboro News and Record published a story on their website that was titled: "Woman Enrolls In Her Own Beauty School." The article tells how Dr. Dudley enrolled in her own beauty school at the tender age of 71! Who does this?

The article reported that Dr. Dudley had never been able to do hair, not even her two daughters' hair. To remedy that, she did what she had to in order to rectify the situation. Her example shows that anyone can pursue their unfulfilled dreams. And, no matter your age, you ***can*** *make your dreams become a reality.*

Dr. Dudley provides us with more than enough inspiration to let our lights shine. What unfilled desire do you have in your heart? Follow after Dr. Dudley's example and stop hiding your light under a bushel. Go after your dream, live out loud, and let your light shine!

Eunice Mosley was born in Selma, Alabama, the seventh of nine children born to Andrew M. Mosley, Sr. and Eva O. Murdoch Mosley. She exhibited a creative spirit and a deep desire to learn at a very early age. In 1960, she started selling Fuller Products door-to-door in Brooklyn, New York, while still a student at Talladega College. That summer, she met Joe L. Dudley, Sr. when they both were selling Fuller Products to earn college tuition money. They married in 1961 and both began working for Fuller Products full-time in 1962.

By 1976, the Dudleys had helped develop a sales force of more than 400 staff, as well as a beauty school and a chain of beauty supply stores located throughout the Southeast. Dudley Products was deemed an entrepreneurial success.

The design, planning and building of Dudley Products, Inc.'s new manufacturing and home office facility in Kernersville, North Carolina, was personally supervised by Dr. Dudley. These efforts earned her the Energy Efficient Building Award, presented by Energy User News. She was also recognized with the ASHRAE Technology Award when she placed second in an international competition touting outstanding achievements in the design and operation of energy-efficient buildings.

Over the past forty years, her hard work has helped the Dudley Q+ Brand achieve international success and acclaim.

In June 2008, Joe and Eunice Dudley restructured the Dudley conglomerate and turned over day-to-day responsibilities to their daughter, Ursula Dudley Oglesby, who created Dudley Beauty Corp, LLC.

In 2009, Joe and Eunice Dudley were featured in Chris Rock's acclaimed documentary about the hair care industry, "Good Hair."

Eunice Dudley strongly believes in giving back to the community. She frequently volunteers her time, money, and resources to various boards and organizations, and has received prestigious recognition for her efforts, such as:

- Board Member for the Community Foundation of Greater Greensboro
- Financial Secretary for Greater Greensboro/Reidsville club of NANPBW
- United Negro College Fund contributor
- Former member of Bennett College Board of Trustees and the NCA&T Board of Trustees
- Former member of Providence Baptist Church Board of Trustees
- Member Direct Selling Education Foundation Board
- NAAWLI Legacy of Leadership awardee in 2008
- Recipient of The Athena Award from the Greensboro Area Chamber of Commerce.
- Recipient of the Crystal Award from the NANBPW Clubs, Inc.
- Co-Winner of The Kernersville First Citizens of The Year Award in 1993
- Awarded an Honorary Doctor of Humane Letters by Bennett College for her business success and for being a role model for young women in the community.

SHINING PAST THE VEIL OF REJECTION

Tanya R. Bankston, MA, CLC, SST

Rejection tears at the fabric of the human soul; sending a message that destroys a woman's self-esteem, self-value, and self-worth.

--Tanya R Bankston

When I think about the fact that my life could have been ended more than forty-nine years ago by a straightened metal clothes hanger inserted into my sixteen-year-old mother's womb, I am grateful that God had another plan!

I haven't always been grateful.

Because my mother wanted to terminate my life, a spirit of rejection seemed to hover over me from birth. One definition of "rejection," as written in the Oxford English Dictionary, reads: "the emotional refusal or inability to accept one's own child; the state of rejecting a child, or of being rejected by a parent." My mother gave birth to me at a time in history when teenagers were not rewarded with reality TV shows for getting pregnant before marriage. She was sheltered, afraid, and misinformed about sexuality. When she told me that she had wanted to abort me, feelings of rage, guilt, and shame engulfed me. In fact, that hovering spirit of rejection caused me to live with these feelings for most of my life.

I wasn't ready for her type of truth. Her blunt honesty was too much reality for my young mind. Her words were a sharpened blade that cut my heart into many pieces. This conversation began as one of our normal mother-daughter bonding sessions, but ended with me feeling a need for emotionally reconstructive surgery. She meant no harm, but her revelation activated dark, tormenting thoughts that swirled within me. I was stunned.

I wondered, "Could my mother ever love me after initially not wanting and rejecting me?"

Because my father wasn't in my life, I also wondered if I was the reason he left. Was I really such a vile and repulsive creature that I drove my father out of my life too?

After the shock of my mother's disclosure, I was in mental agony. My tortured mind relentlessly accused me...and I had one main thought:

"Why did God create such a hideous creature like me?"

Growing up, the deep root of rejection made me feel inadequate, unaccepted, and incomplete. Rejection made me feel I never fit in, that I was out of place in every setting. I always felt my presence wasn't welcome, because I constantly heard messages of rejection everywhere I went that stained my soul.

"You are too thin."
"You are so black."
"You look like that creature from the black lagoon."
"You are a pretty girl to be SO BLACK!"
"Your feet are too big!"

I heard these negative descriptions of myself so often that I cried all the time. I constantly felt sad and depressed because I was rejected by my peers, my father, and my mother. These internal and external messages stung me to my core.

When I look back, I marvel that I did not develop into a sadistic serial killer or die from my many suicide attempts. But now I see it was obvious that God had other plans for my life.

My rejection was affirmed repeatedly until puberty knocked at my door. I was still black and thin, but I gained two new attractive friends: my breasts! At first, I really enjoyed having breasts. But even they contributed to my sense of rejection because of the overwhelming and unsolicited attention they brought me. I was one of the first girls in my neighborhood to develop breasts. After that, I suddenly became popular with the guys in the neighborhood.

The budding of my breasts and the curve of my hips gave me a newfound courage to seek the acceptance and approval I craved from my newly attentive male suitors. Part of me enjoyed this new attention, while a deeper part of me understood that it was only temporary. However, I didn't care how temporary this male attention was; it felt good to be sought after and desired. Sadly, this attention turned harmful when I became the victim of repeated sexual abuse.

The first time I was molested, I followed the rules: I immediately told an adult what happened to me. After I did that, I thought I would be protected. I thought I would be believed. I thought someone would speak up for me, and comfort me. But my attempt to do the right thing was rebuffed and my lifelong message of rejection was reinforced.

The next time I was assaulted was different. I was approached by a male acquaintance of my family who said he would pay me if I let him fondle my breasts. On one level, I knew that letting him do this to me was wrong; but I overrode my inner good judgment and rationalized that it would be okay because he offered me twenty-five dollars. Since I didn't have a job or a regular allowance, this seemed like an appropriate sum to let him fondle me. Here I was at the tender age of twelve negotiating a sexual deal. I justified my actions by thinking of it as a purely business deal. I had breasts, which he wanted. He had money, which I wanted. Making that deal on my own terms quickly taught me the influence of my sexuality on men, and I wanted to capitalize on it. In my young and unformed mind, it was a perfect win/win for both of us. However, after this episode, I hesitated to tell another adult...because this man was allegedly an "adult." After this experience, a seed was planted inside me that adults could not be trusted. My innocence was ravaged and my virtue was shattered.

Because of these encounters, I believed the only type of love or physical affection I deserved involved giving away my virtue. I rationalized that I wasn't hurting myself, but I was very wrong. It would take me decades to understand the impact that these sexual negotiations had on me...spiritually, psychologically, emotionally, and physically. The veil of shame over how I let myself be treated cast me into a deep depression and threatened to dim my radiance and sparkle forever. But just as God had plans for me other than being aborted, He also had a greater plan to unearth the brilliance that lay dormant within me.

I rededicated my life to Christ. Once I did, God began to fill my spirit with His presence and power. He gave me words to meditate on, and they helped facilitate my healing. The black veil that had covered me my entire life lifted as I meditated on the words the Holy Spirit poured into me. For decades, I felt as if the letter "R" for "Rejection" was branded on my soul. God's words of truth counteracted the negative feelings of rejection within me. As a result, I adopted new "R" words: Restoration, Rejuvenation, Renew, Recharge, Recreate, Refocus, Realignment, Revive, Reflection, Reconnection, Rejoice, Revitalize, Reposition, Reinvention, and Redeemed. As I began speaking to others about my life, I was transformed from REsisting God to being REsilient through God. My hope for the future was REstored and my brilliance was unearthed as I allowed God to transform my thoughts, my speech, and my actions.

I made the decision that 2009 would be the year I would purge all my past hurt, but I have to be totally honest. In the beginning, dealing head on with my past was very difficult. I had experienced so much pain at the hands of men that I still had real difficulty trusting God to not hurt me, too. But I was determined to believe that He had more than enough power to love me. I decided I would trust that He understood all I had gone through and would not negatively judge me for my past actions. I believed that my every experience, good and bad, could be used by Him for a greater purpose. Ironically, during that year, I sometimes still expected God to lie...just like other men in my life had done. But His Word promised me that it is impossible for Him to lie. I began to trust and understand that He is not a man, and therefore, He cannot lie.

The more I came to realize how much God loved me, the more I understood that my earlier feelings of inadequacy did not come from Him. As I continued to meditate on the Word of God, all the dark feelings of shame, guilt, unforgiveness, and bitterness began to melt away.

I began walking with my head held high! As it says in God's Word, I exchanged beauty for ashes, the oil of joy for mourning, and the garment of praise for the spirit of heaviness.

I also found the courage to tell my story. As I began to speak my truth and share my experiences with other women, I learned that my story of sexual abuse, shame, and guilt is not unique. Other women also suffer the same pain and walk covered with the same veil of darkness. Women constantly share stories of their abuse; and I am amazed at how the characters change but the story is similar (or identical) to mine. I encourage those sisters who still suffer in silence to allow their sparkle to shine.

Over time, God helped me step outside of my comfort zone and into a new life. I eventually graduated from college, changed careers, got married, and started a business.

I want you to know that the victory of my transformation is also available to you. You can rise from the depths of despair, rejection, guilt, and shame. You can throw off the muck and mire you feel covers you. I also used to feel trampled and discarded under the muck of a supremely unhappy life. My only prayer as a young woman was to be loved and accepted.

Today I am a woman who shines. I have learned to walk in authenticity and I am no longer afraid of rejection's sting. Thanks to my Heavenly Father, I sparkle and glisten. I know now that my worth is more valuable than rubies. I wear strength and honor as my clothing rather than the rags of rejection.

I freely share my story with you. I encourage you to trust the God I serve. Don't feel it's too difficult for Him to change your life. I know that God will pull you up from rejection to a place of clarity and grace. He can and will pull the veil of darkness off you.

I am still being polished. I am still in the process of discovering my beauty and knowing my worth. But I know that I will forever continue to shine.

> *The raggedy rejected pieces of my soul have been woven into a shining cloak of beauty and grace. God used every strand of thread for His Glory.*
>
> *--Tanya R Bankston*

Tanya Bankston, SST, BS, MAS, CLC is a Certified Life, Leadership & Solutions Focused Coach who embraces the concept that Leadership, Excellence in Customer Service, and Personal Empowerment are the staples of life for all aspects of a positive "Quality of Life."

In an effort to foster motivation, inspiration and value to the lives of others, Mrs. Bankston has served in the capacities of Professional Life & Leadership Coach, Contributing Author & Accomplished Speaker for various Association Conferences and Seminars. Find additional information at www.coachtbankston.com.

THE ONE THING

Anita Newby

At the age of twenty-nine, I became an orphan.

Certainly, that sounds unusual. Some people envision orphans as infants being raised by a group of nuns in isolated, rural locations. Others see orphans as red-headed pre-teens who sing songs and dance dances with their inexplicably talented, parentless housemates, as in the musical *Annie.* Regardless of the picture in your mind, you most likely did not envision me. But by definition, that is exactly what I had become; an orphan...a child whose parents were dead.

My mother was Kay. My father was James. She was a beautiful, vibrant First Lady and a compassionate woman who untiringly demonstrated the love of God to anyone who would receive it...and even to those who would not. He was a wise, humble, gentle Pastor who passionately and graciously cared for and covered his family and his flock in the same manner I imagine that Jesus would. To others, they were viewed as role models, teachers, leaders, counselors, and pillars of the community. To me, the youngest of their five children, they were simply Mama and Daddy...and that was everything.

They were my first encounter with true love. They showed me what it meant to love God and to live for Him without restriction and without restraint. They handled hardships with grace and faith. They forgave quickly. They loved deeply. They were my protection and provision; my safety and stability. They instilled in me ideals that allowed me to live life confidently, boldly and on purpose. Because of them, I was fearless, I was faith-filled, and I had the freedom to be uniquely me. But one day, they were no longer there and the foundation upon which I built the tenets of my existence was shaken.

I recognize the blessing of not being orphaned as a young child. I had the benefit of their tutelage throughout my formative years and beyond. I was legally and technically an adult when my parents passed. They did not pass away simultaneously. My mother's death preceded my father's by 10 years. When he died, I awakened to the reality of an unfamiliar and undesirable truth: I was now an orphan.

My newfound realization was accompanied by a strange dichotomy of feelings. On one hand, I felt uncertain, abandoned, rejected, uncovered, vulnerable, and lost. As a single woman with no children or parents, what was I to do? Who would help me? Who would guide me? Who would simply care for me? On the other hand, I felt a sense of duty, responsibility, purpose, and drive. My parents may have been gone, but I was still here. I was determined to maximize my existence and live out my purpose. But what exactly was my purpose? Therein lay my dilemma.

My siblings and I were raised in quite a balanced environment. Yes, we were the children of a pastor, but our upbringing was neither legalistic nor restrictive. Certainly, we were somewhat sheltered and had clear-cut boundaries, but we were not hidden from the world. We were exposed to many amazing and perhaps unconventional experiences that shaped our worldview. We went to movies. We listened to every type of music available. We frequented sporting events. We attended live theater and went to museums. We heard orchestras. We traveled by plane, train, and automobile. We took family vacations that did not involve attending a church conference, convention, or convocation. We accomplished this and much more while still attending church four to five times a week...which made for a beautiful balance. God was always first in our lives and we lived passionately for Him. But we were able to see and experience Him outside of the conventional functionality of the church.

Being exposed to such a variety of experiences unearthed a myriad of personal passions within me. I had always been drawn to ministry. After all, it was in my DNA. Without question, that would always be a huge part of my life. My family was also musically inclined. I could not imagine a world where I didn't make music. I had career goals. I had personal goals. Suffice it to say, I wasn't interested in only one thing, and I wasn't good at only one thing. But I desperately wanted to do *the one thing* for which God had designed me. After all, He created me for a purpose, right?

While struggling to identify the one thing God planted me on earth to do, I began to receive mixed messages. I had been in ministry for years and had taken steps to distance myself from those possessing and propagating antiquated views of women's roles; so my struggle was not whether I would be recognized because I was a woman. My struggle involved how far could I go as a young single woman? Certain titles could only be obtained if accompanied by an AARP card or a husband. I had neither. Though these requirements were not written, they were clearly the standard.

I have a degree in music and have invested time, energy, and money into perfecting that gift. So what message do I ascertain when a trusted ministry leader and mentor tells me that my season for music has ended?

I was told: "Don't worry about singing. Just focus on your ministry."

Questions flooded my mind: "If God doesn't want me to sing, will He reimburse me for this degree?" "If I can't sing here, can I sing elsewhere? Oh, I forgot. That's not allowed. Only what happens inside the four walls of this church is sanctioned by God."

Fortunately, I asked none of these sarcastic questions out loud. But that internal conversation caused me to wonder: "What is my passion?"

Though theater has always been a part of my life, I have performed in theatrical events more consistently within the past ten years. Several years ago, I was privileged enough (or perhaps crazy enough) to work on two plays concurrently. One was a classic Disney musical and the other was a riveting, original Christian drama.

During my preparation for the shows, a church mother approached me regarding my involvement. She posed a deep, religious question.

She asked, "Which one of these plays is most important?"

Well, I already knew where this was going, so I replied, "The Disney show. I have an opportunity to meet and work with people that may not know Christ. I can be an example. I can be a light."

She quickly corrected me. "No! The most important one is the Christian play because it's about God."

And once again, I received another mixed message. Was the non-Christian play a waste of time? Did God not open that door of opportunity for me?

I continued in ministry even as I indulged in my passion for the theater. Concurrently, I also held various leadership positions in church and was ordained as a pastor. Simultaneously, I was also working with different local theaters and pursued training to further cultivate my artistic abilities. But I still questioned what my true passion was. Was using my gift for all things theatrical really what God intended for me? Was I distracted by so-called "worldly desire"? If I have more than one vision, does that create division? These were the messages I wrestled to resolve.

After a strenuous season of ministry, I took a step back and reduced my ministry involvement. I was tired, wounded, and discouraged. I submerged myself in theater life...a life I loved and a life that loved me in return. I was performing in shows back-to-back and was away from my home an average of fifteen hours a day during the workweek. It was physically tiring, yet also refreshing and rewarding. But in the depths of my soul, another passion reignited that had been heretofore dimmed: the art of worship. I wanted to lead people into God's presence through music and His Word. I wanted to see people walk in the freedom Jesus had purchased for them. I wanted God's people to be empowered to impact and influence the world. I had a glimpse of where God wanted to take me in ministry and how it was to be executed.

Knowing that there is safety in a multitude of counsellors, I began to share my thoughts with a few select individuals. Their responses were generally favorable, but I needed more. I needed an action plan for my next steps, for mentoring and accountability. So, I sought the counsel of a wise, trustworthy, seasoned leader who I felt would assuredly provide the guidance I needed and desired. During our meeting, I shared with her a bit of my background and disclosed my heart concerning ministry. Much to my surprise, my ideas were assailed and my ministry desires were discouraged. My qualifications were questioned. My experience was invalidated, and worst of all, my will was broken. I was encouraged to redirect my energy toward the stage. The will that I was in the process of mending was once again a victim of friendly fire.

Let me clarify. The meeting did produce some favorable results. As the conversation progressed, the leader began to see the full scope of my non-traditional ministry approach and offered additional insight. Even though she continued to steer me away from the church as my calling, she provided practical action steps to achieve my goals. I walked away with a plan in my hand, but confusion in my heart. I was back to wrestling with finding my one true thing. I entered the meeting broken and vulnerable; I departed in an even weaker emotional state, and the action steps she gave me felt irrelevant.

For weeks, I struggled to take the necessary steps I needed to reach my goals. I struggled to pray. I struggled to be motivated to do more than my daily obligations. Once, I had an identity that had been clearly established and solidified by God and my parents. But through the course of mixed messages, religious rhetoric and the friendly fire I was receiving, I once again felt lost, abandoned and alone. This is what it's like for orphans.

Not long after this feeling of uselessness had taken residence in my heart, I heard God speak to me while sitting on my couch. The message was short and sweet.

He simply said, "You are equal parts James and equal parts Kay."

I stopped for a moment. I wasn't sure what I had heard. Was I hallucinating? It wasn't an audible voice, but it was definitely clear. But what did it mean?

As quickly as that thought penetrated my mind, God downloaded this message into my spirit:

"You have equal passions for ministry and theater because you are a product of both James and Kay...in equal parts. He loved ministry and she loved the theater. She chose to step away from theater for ministry and family. That was her choice; you do not have to choose. You can do both and even more. Your passions are not in conflict. They are in concert. I haven't called you to just one thing. Your DNA contains more than one thing. Your heritage consists of more than one thing. Your parents' legacy is about more than one thing. You do not have to choose."

Immediately, a wave of freedom enveloped me. The pressure I had put on myself to choose one thing over the other had lifted. I was not bound by a singular purpose. And personally, I do not believe that God, in His vastness, creates anything with a singular purpose. We are made in the image of a multi-faceted God so we should reflect that truth accordingly.

Think about our greatest example: Jesus. He is more than "One Thing." He is 100% God and yet 100% man. He was a rabbi and a carpenter. He is Alpha and Omega, the beginning and the ending. God never has and never will be a one-trick pony, so why should I be?

Now think about the women you know, including yourself. Without effort and without thought, you are equipped to effectively accomplish multiple things, yet you are constantly being told through words or actions to stay in your lane...or reprioritize your values...or be content with where you are.

Those messages alone are not erroneous, but when delivered without insight or foresight into who you really are, they can extinguish your light.

Do not make the same mistakes I made. You cannot expect external sources to ignite and affirm your passions. Know that the key to your brilliance is in your genetic make-up, both naturally and spiritually. Do not let the viewpoints, opinions, and insecurities of others influence your pursuits. You are not one thing! You cannot be contained by a singular purpose or platform. You are bigger than that. You are bolder than that. You are brighter than that!

Take some time and pull away from the voices. Get alone with your Creator, and allow His voice to be the spark that helps you redefine and rediscover your identity. Silence the mixed messages from those who only know a portion of your potential. Shut your ears to the religious rhetoric that serves only to reduce your radiance. Drive back the friendly fire and move forward in the many facets of your purpose.

This orphan, who struggled to find a singular purpose, is now free to pursue multiple passions and live out her parents' legacy. No longer will I allow religious perspectives to dim my light. No longer will I let others impose their paths on me. No longer will mixed messages confuse and frustrate my purposes. I am free to rest in the multiplicity of my natural and spiritual DNA. I am free to shine!

Anita Newby is an accomplished singer, vocal instructor, worship leader, public speaker, pastor, and organizational leader. She is also an actress whose passion for all things artistic permeates every aspect of her life. She holds a Bachelor's Degree in Music from Wayne State University in Detroit, Michigan. Her vocal skills, as well as songwriting abilities, have been displayed on numerous recordings. She is a credit union executive, specializing in coaching and training. She flows with an undeniable prophetic anointing and is dedicated to advancing the kingdom of God through multiple spheres of influence. Contact her at akaynewby@gmail.com or find her at https://www.facebook.com/AnitaNewbySings/

FINDING MY VOICE

Tiara Curry

The words I heard were clearly directed towards me. It was a message straight from heaven to my heart; a message that would rouse me out of a place of fear, lethargy and complacency into a place of action. I received this message shortly after I'd delivered Zion, my sixth child. I was holding her in my lap while watching a DVD from a conference my husband had recently attended.

"There is someone's salvation and deliverance attached to you walking in the full measure of the purpose for which I have destined you. Their success is contingent upon you. I put you here to release power to set a people free. Walk in the measure, power, and purpose I have called you to."

After I watched the video, "Yes, Lord" was my response to that sacred encounter. Before watching that video, I had already made the decision to step out of the background and begin to move in what God called me to do: be a voice in this world and in His Kingdom. Once I heard that word on the video and accepted that it was for me, the war began. There was a fight to dim the anointing and the shine that God placed within me. No one else dimmed my shine...it was I who was doing the dimming. You dim your own shine when you do not rise to the call that has been placed upon your life.

In my journey to do God's bidding, there were many forces and battles that would not let me shine. There was the battle of balance. There were concerns as to whether my family and home would be okay if I turned my attention away from them and focused more on my ministry. There was the battle of wondering if it was really my time to move, because I already had so much on my plate. There was the struggle to allow my husband to be the main voice while I remained in the background. I also had questions like: "Is this really my season, or should I wait until my children are older?" The enemy of my destiny was relentless in his pursuit to keep me backed into a corner and hidden from the light.

In spite of these obstacles, I began to receive ideas to bring my purpose to fruition. However, I did not immediately act on them. I was operating somewhat in my calling, but not in the full measure of it. I'd started a ministry alongside my husband, had been ordained, and was leading a ministry for women and children. However, I was not doing all that God had instructed me to do because of fear. I was afraid of failure. I feared that everything would be too much...too overwhelming. I would shrink back and sit instead of rising to the call. I had to fight to rise above everyone and everything that told me I was not strong enough, brilliant enough or adequate enough.

The voice of doubt screamed in my head: "No one wants to hear from you!" "Someone else is better for the task." "There are so many people already doing what you're doing."

After a time, I really began to feel that I wouldn't make a difference; because those voices compelled me to be content to stay in the background and never come into the spotlight.

My husband would say, "You have a voice, Tiara. People need to hear it."

I knew I had to find a way to let go of the fear and the inner voices that spoke a very loud "no!" each time I tried to move forward.

I believe this gut-wrenching fear started in my childhood. I remember being teased and ridiculed because of my clothing and the way I spoke. I can also remember the teacher calling my name in class to answer a question. When I answered wrong, I was laughed at by my classmates. I remember being chased around the gated playground during recess. The enemy is very cunning and strategic. He already knows the greatness that resides in you, so he tries to stifle it at an early age. His goal is to make you believe you are powerless. He uses fear to grip you and make you run and hide. Fear dims you. Fear makes you invisible. Fear keeps you covered up from the light that shines. Think of your fears. Ask God to show you what you are afraid of. Ask Him to help you walk through your fears. In order to truly shine, you have to face your fears and walk through them. "Do it afraid!" That's my new motto!

Never let fear reach a point where it keeps you from being brave. You can't be afraid of learning new things or discovering what you are capable of. As your thoughts change, you'll begin to see what "FEAR" really means. F.E.A.R. is another way of saying: "False Evidence that Appears Real." To combat fear, you must come from a place of hiding to a place where you are uncovered and able to receive the light. And, as you allow that light to shine upon you, you are strengthened by an ability to move forward.

In my life, I was afflicted with "perfect moment" syndrome. It became my habit to buy things but wait for the "perfect moment" to use or indulge in it. For example, I'd buy a few ounces of loose leaf tea, or some chocolate. Instead of savoring them after I'd bought them, I'd wait for a "perfect moment" to enjoy them. I bought books and waited for the "perfect moment" to read them. But I am just about delivered from this syndrome. I now know that a "perfect moment" is whatever moment you decide is perfect...you don't have to wait. If you are waiting on your own "perfect moment," I encourage you to make that moment now.

In order to shake myself out of my "perfect moment" syndrome and silence the voices that spoke very loudly against me, I began to write affirmations and prayers in my journals. I wanted to rise to the challenge God placed before me. I took time to revisit the prophecies, prayers, and dreams I'd been given throughout my life. These simple acts helped me change my thinking and move closer to the light.

Because I believe that we must write and post words that affirm us and remind us of who we are, I am the queen of writing on Post-it™ notes. I wrote the words "I refuse to fear" on one note. I wrote "God's grace is sufficient for me" on another note. And I also wrote other affirmations:

> "I am not inadequate."
> "I will not be intimidated."
> "The Lord is on my side; I will not fear."

I posted these notes in places where I could see and speak them regularly. I placed them anywhere I would be reminded that there is a place for my voice to be heard. I posted them in hallway closets, on the walls of my home, even in my car. I wrote and posted affirmations on every mirror. And the funny thing is, whenever I'd have visitors over, they would begin to read and say those things too!

Another thing I began to do was speak into the atmosphere. Whether it was a quote, a meme, scripture, or a positive affirmation, I would speak it out of my mouth. The practical act of speaking is very powerful and helps motivate me into action. Hearing positive words spoken out loud helps build my self-confidence. The act of speaking gives me the power I need to move forward.

One of my favorite affirmations was penned by self-help guru Marianne Williamson, who wrote:

> *"Our deepest fear is not that we are inadequate. Our deepest fear is that we are powerful beyond measure. It is our light, not our darkness that most frightens us. We ask ourselves, 'Who am I to be brilliant, gorgeous, talented, and fabulous?' Actually, who are you not to be? You are a child of God. Your playing small does not serve the world. There is nothing enlightened about shrinking so that other people won't feel insecure around you. We are all meant to shine, as children do. We were born to make manifest the glory of God that is within us. It's not just in some of us; it's in everyone. And as we let our own light shine, we unconsciously give other people permission to do the same. As we are liberated from our own fear, our presence automatically liberates others."*

The first time I saw her quote was while watching the movie "Akeelah And The Bee." For some reason, this quote has stuck with me for years. I now use her words as a reminder to allow my light to shine. Her words were the motivation I needed to move from the background into God's spotlight.

Each one of us has some special quality that we need to share with the world. Whatever God has called you to do, I encourage you to take whatever steps He tells you in order to be successful. He will lead and guide you, but you must do the work. What do you feel God is calling you to do? What do you believe is your purpose on this earth? Are you operating in it?

After overcoming fear, and being empowered to move, I asked the Lord for wisdom to launch the ministry He'd given me. I know that He has more to do in and through me in order for my light to truly shine. I am longer hidden in the background. I am taking steps toward launching the ministry

God has entrusted to me. Now that I am taking steps to launch it, people have begun to offer help. This is where my real joy lies: I know that the more I silence negative thoughts and feelings and begin to move, God will bring people into my life to help fulfill my vision.

Are you hiding? Are you running from the very thing you should be running to?

I speak directly to you: "Come out of the darkness!"

You have so much more inside you than you realize. It is not too late to begin operating in your purpose. This book has been sent as a prophetic message...to enable you to rise and shine because your Light has come. God is calling you to come forth and impact the world with your gifts. I declare that you are leaving your place of obscurity. You will come from a place of complacency and fear and you will walk in a place of faith. Believe that you are valuable. Break through every limitation and allow the Light of Christ to rise up in you. When you do not rise up to be the authentic person that you were created to be, you do a disservice to those around you. People need what you have to offer.

I encourage you to find your voice and use it for whatever you have been created for. What dreams and passions do you have inside you? Maybe you were created to start a school. Maybe you are supposed to open a new medical practice. Maybe you were created to launch a business. Find out what your purpose is and identify what's been holding you back from achieving it. Do not let outside influences keep you from walking in your purpose. Refuse to listen to any voice that tries to silence you. Do whatever it takes to reach your goal. Operate in your purpose. Show up, show out, and give your all to what God has called you to do. Overcome every challenge you face and then you will be that light that shines so brightly for others to see.

Wife, mother, and friend are just a few words that describe Tiara Curry, pastor of Life Changers Church in Cincinnati, Ohio. A native of Detroit, Tiara has always had a heart for helping people. She is passionate about mentoring women, helping them to move from where they are to where God has called them to be. By using examples from her own life, she empowers women to find their purpose and walk in it. Tiara finds joy in serving alongside her husband Warren in ministry. They have been married for sixteen years and are the proud parents of six children.

WATER YOUR OWN GARDEN

Zabrina Gordon

As women, we tend to lose our identities because we identify more with our roles as daughters, sisters, mothers, wives, and caregivers. However, what about our own needs? What happens to us as individuals if our needs are not met? Why do we get lost in all the chaos we call life? Why do we forget about ourselves? I can't answer these questions for everyone, but I'm sure many can relate to my story of emotional and mental turmoil. In times of crisis, I try to bear the burdens and sorrows of those I hold dear and ignore my own grief and heartbreak. Over the last four years, I have lost more people than I care to count. While I cherish all those I have lost, my most personally devastating losses were the murder of my only child, and suffering through the horror and pain of watching cancer slowly ravage my dear sister and best friend.

Let me begin my story by sharing that my only child came into this world as my sister's first-born son. I was there for him from the day he was born and loved him as if he had been formed in my own womb. He was the apple of my eye and we had a unique bond. While I didn't know at the time that I would later adopt him, I know now that it was predestined. My beloved sister loved me so much that she gave me the greatest gift: motherhood. Words cannot begin to express the joy and gratitude I felt as I nurtured and cared for him and watched him grow. I knew I loved him deeply, but I didn't know the intensity of that love until the ill-fated day I received a devastating phone call that my son had been shot. Nothing can describe the fear that rocked my soul. As panic flowed through my body, I called a close friend to confirm whether or not my baby was dead or alive. While I was waiting for news, I prayed to God for the best outcome. But even so, I knew in my heart that my son was gone. When I received solid confirmation of his death, I was numb.

I found myself audibly saying to God, "I don't understand. This is not right! Why my baby?"

I cried all night long in disbelief. My spirit was broken and my heart was in a million pieces. But still, I did what I do best...bury my pain and work on making things right for everybody else. I also had to plan my son's funeral. I called my family to see how everyone was holding up. I encouraged them to be strong. I reassured them that we would all make it through this difficult time. I arrived in Milwaukee, my hometown, on autopilot. I blocked my own grief and carried the weight of my family's sorrow, because I am known as "The Fixer" in my family. While no one ever asked me to take on this role, I always felt it was my responsibility to fix everything...even things that could never be repaired. Though I was hurting, I put aside my pain and focused on my family. I knew a bit of the magnitude of the pain they felt because my son was everybody's favorite.

I did everything humanly possible to ease the pain of my loved ones. I arranged a visit for my mother, sister, and I to go to the morgue. As I looked down on my beloved son's remains, the moment was surreal. It was as if someone else was lying there cold and lifeless. The reality of his death didn't really register at that time. I made it through the funeral and burial with unbelievable strength. It wasn't until I returned to

Atlanta that my grief hit me like a ton of bricks. I couldn't sleep, eat, or breathe. I felt like I was choking.

I sat in my room and cried out to God, "Why him? Why my baby?"

I told the Lord, "I just don't understand! I need you to speak to me, Jesus. Father, show me the silver lining in this untimely loss."

I was shaken to my core. I knew God was there, but my faith was shaky because of my loss and the nonstop questions spiraling through my head. I spoke to God this way for two days, while my husband did all he could to console me. On the third day, I woke up and checked my email. I saw a note saying I had received a free book titled, "Surprised by Suffering: The Role of Pain and Death in the Life of a Christian" by R.C. Sproul. The story that struck me most was of a distraught father who was deeply grieved over the death of his son.

The man sought counsel from his pastor and asked: "Where was God when my son died?' In response, the pastor calmly said, "The same place He was when His son died."

While I was still devastated and hurt because of my loss, reading that story made me realize I didn't have to be in despair. I was reminded of the hope I had in Jesus Christ. Reading the story reminded me that my weeping was normal and my grief was part of a season that I had to endure. I was determined to go through my sorrow by faith. I surrendered to my grief and to the Holy Spirit. I gained comfort and strength through my tears and memories. I was able to move forward, knowing the truth of 1 Thessalonians 4:13-14 (GNT): "*Our friends, we want you to know the truth about those who have died, so that you will not be sad, as are those who have no hope.* [14]*We believe that Jesus died and rose again, and so we believe that God will take back with Jesus those who have died believing in him."*

Though I continued to grieve, I slowly began to change. I was no longer as angry or irritated as a result of my loss. I found comfort in cherishing the memories and the time I shared with my beloved son.

Approximately three months into my healing process, I was thrown off balance again when my sister was diagnosed with Stage 4 colon cancer with liver metastasis. Once again, I sprang into action to fix the problem. Certainly, I would not lose my sister and best friend so soon after the traumatic loss of my child. I went to support my sister, not knowing what to expect. When I reviewed her medical records and spoke with her doctors, the prognosis was poor. Initially, I pleaded with God to make the cancer disappear and heal her body. I prayed for God to extend her life. While I was standing strong in my faith, I was reminded that there is a time and season for all things. Although she showed signs of improvement and even went into remission for a short time, I knew God was preparing me for the greater task of letting her go. I prayed for God's strength to be able to accept whatever His will would be for my sister's life...as well as my own. During this time, I was studying to become a chaplain; and several times, I wondered why I was drawn to this ministry. Later, I could see that God had a plan.

While caring for my sister, I wept often...even during those times when she seemed to be doing fine. Through my tears, little did I know that God was preparing me for the difficult task that lay ahead. I would talk to my husband about my fear that my sister was slipping away. He said that she looked fine and reassured me that she would be okay. I told him empathically that she was dying. There were late nights and early mornings when the Holy Spirit would prompt me to encourage and comfort her during her most difficult moments. I would call her and stay on the phone until she could relax and drift off to sleep. One morning when I called, she was not doing well and had to be hospitalized. I called to tell her that I was coming home. She told me she had prayed to God that He would send me. After I arrived, I stayed at the hospital with her day and night. During the late hours of the night, I climbed in bed with her and held her tight. I reassured her that I wouldn't leave her alone. During this time, it became clear that she wasn't going to make it, so I brought her back home with me to Atlanta. During that time, God used me to care for her. In fact, we were both being prepared by Him for her transition home.

As I said, I didn't understand why God called me to become a chaplain. But shortly after my sister's passing, He revealed His reasons to me. As I was taking care of her during her illness, I saw that the chaplaincy, like caregiving, is a ministry of presence. Not only did caring for my sister prepare me to simply listen to her wants, needs, desires, and fears, it taught me to be fully present in the moment without distractions. Helping her also taught me to be present with myself. I learned that sometimes I needed to water my own garden. What do I mean when I say, "water my own garden"? Watering your own garden simply means taking time for yourself without feeling guilty...no matter what is going on in life. It's all about self-care. You must nurture yourself spiritually, mentally, and physically.

When there were quiet moments during my caring for my sister, I learned to just sit and listen to God and replenish my spirit. I learned to listen to myself and take notice of my needs from a holistic (physically, spiritually, mentally) standpoint. When I was busy pouring out my spirit to my sister, my family and others, I often forgot to take a breather just for myself. In the midst of taking care of others, I dismissed my own needs. I masked my hurts, my fears, my insecurities, my sadness, and my anxiety. After all (I reasoned), I am a strong, mature Christian who has it all together. I was afraid to let others down. I felt guilty for stepping away from situations and from people who needed me. God showed me that I cannot do anything without Him, because my shoulders aren't broad enough to carry everyone. He showed me that I could do all things through Him...especially the tasks He specifically assigned to me. I encourage you right now to take some quality time for yourself. Doing so will better equip you to help others. Remember to take time to sit before God and listen for His guidance. When life becomes overwhelming, take time to stop and water your garden.

To water your garden, start with simple things. Set a regular bedtime for yourself. Limit phone calls after a certain time of the evening. Have a cup of tea or coffee. As you take sips, notice the flavor, the feel and the warmth of the beverage as it goes down. Enjoy and savor the moment! Go for a short walk. Pause for a moment to observe the beauty of nature. Listen to the sounds of birds chirping. Hear the wind rustling in the trees. Feel the warmth of the sun touching your face. Sit for a minute and flip through your favorite magazine...or read a book that you've been meaning to get to, but never seem to find time for. Even though this will cost you nothing, you will gain something very valuable: A "peace" of your time. You're worth it! Be mindful! Get a massage or facial. Treat yourself to dinner or a movie. Go on a retreat. Meditate by sitting silently and reconnecting with yourself. Get clarity on who you are and what you want out of life. Really meditate on your likes and dislikes. Reevaluate those dreams that you placed on hold because of other responsibilities. Focus on ways to bring those dreams and desires to fruition. You will be better able to help those you love and encourage others in need when you water your own garden. Just as a natural garden requires attention to yield its crops, you also must nurture your soul, your spirit, and your body in order to illuminate the beauty within you. When you take time to allow yourself to rest, refresh, replenish, and renew, then you will truly SHINE!

Zabrina Gordon currently resides in the Metro Atlanta area with her husband of fifteen years, Derrick. She is a board-certified Christian Counselor, Chaplain, Ordained Minister, and published author, including the anthology, "IT'S POSSIBLE: Living Beyond Limitations!" She is a graduate of Oglethorpe University with a Bachelor's Degree in Organizational Management and Psychology. She is working towards a Master's in Christian Counseling at Newburgh Theological Seminary and Bible College. She can be reached at counselfromtheheart@gmail.com or (678) 203-6301.

SHINING IN THE LIGHT: A DESIGNER'S ORIGINAL

Pastor Darlene Thorne, M.Div.

Dark Chocolate! I love dark chocolate! I know it has great health properties and it is a powerful source of antioxidants. Dark chocolate may even improve blood flow and lower blood pressure as well. Dark chocolate is usually thought of as being a good thing. Yet, unfortunately, everyone doesn't necessarily like every *type* of dark chocolate. The dark chocolate you eat that tastes so good and that is good for you apparently is not thought of as something good in terms of my complexion. For example, God created my skin the color of dark chocolate, and He created me in His image after His likeness. But because of the rich darkness of my skin color, I was harassed at school for the way God made me.

I used to wonder: "How could God do such a thing to one of His creations?" I felt very alone in this struggle. It seemed no one in my family could see what effect this dilemma was having on me. I did not "get it." What was wrong with the color of my skin? It seemed the more I tried to be invisible, the more I was teased. My personality at home was so different from when I was in school. I became a person who just wanted to hide and be left alone. Not that I did not want to be bothered by people; no, I wanted to have real friends and good relationships. But because all I endured was ridicule and taunting, I would rather not engage in any interaction with those folks. I was also very moody at home. I was the youngest girl, and getting along with my family was less than pleasant. I did not feel like I mattered, so I made poor choices. I would talk back to my mother and was disrespectful to her. I was more afraid of the girls at school than I was of my own mother. But really, I was angry with myself, because I did not know how to deal with the ridicule I faced on a daily basis. It was a difficult thing for me as a child...to be unable to successfully combat unfamiliar forces. Looking back at my childhood, I can see where I was very naïve about many things. I was gullible and really wanted everybody to like me. I was willing to do whatever was necessary to be accepted...not realizing that the more I tried to fit in, the more I did not. Now I know I was not designed to fit in, because it was never a part of God's plan for me to blend into the crowd.

> Psalm 139:14-16 (NIV) says, "*For you created my inmost being; you knit me together in my mother's womb. I praise you because I am fearfully and wonderfully made; your works are wonderful I know that full well. My frame was not hidden from you when I was made in the secret place, when I was woven together in the depths of the earth. Your eyes saw my unformed body; all the days ordained for me were written in your book before one of them came to be.*"

I remember reading this passage of scripture and thinking: "That sounds good, but I am not experiencing the joy of how I was made." I questioned why I looked different from my mother and other siblings.

As a teen, I reflected on how I should dress for school. I did a mental checklist on what I had in my closet. The main colors were navy blue, black, dark brown and forest green. I would not be caught dead wearing any bright colors. My clothes were meant to hide me from any negative attention because they were not flashy. I also presented a happy façade to steer attention away from myself in the hopes that I'd be left alone and not teased for at least one day. Rather than walking around being mad or coming on strong, I put on a false front of being happy. I think I prayed every day that those girls would just leave me alone. During the day at school, I would try to fly under the radar with clothing that was plain and unfashionable. It was a daily struggle to even want to go to school. I felt that, since I had to go, I just wanted to be at peace...so I wore things that would not draw attention to me. However, whatever I wore seemed to do just the opposite. I tried to hide, but it only caused the unwanted attention to heighten to the point where I hated school. I lived for the weekends!

My father was a pastor and our family would travel with him when he was asked to preach. Two things I enjoyed most when we were at the various churches was singing and listening to my dad preach. He was a powerful preacher. He was very studious and would dig deep into the scriptures. I remember one time when we had Bible study and he did an entire teaching based on one word: "NOW!" I know that what my dad instilled in me about the Word of God is the reason I am following in his footsteps as a minister of the Gospel.

My sisters and I were known as the "3D's" because our names are Debbie, Denise and Darlene. We sang wherever our dad preached. I could get lost in singing. Today, all three of us are worship leaders at our various churches because singing never left us. Singing was one of my escapes. That was something I did well and I knew it. No one could take that from me...or so I thought.

One would think that once I became an adult, I could put behind me all the childhood shenanigans that took place in middle school and high school. However, unless or until a person is healed by the power of Holy Spirit, that pain is carried inside them. I found this to be true when I went to college. I brought with me my same belief system that I was not accepted and had to do whatever it took to fit in. I was not teased, but because healing never took place, I had not learned how to trust people. I always thought people had an ulterior motive behind what they said to me, and so I felt I could never let my guard down.

If a person seemed like they genuinely wanted to embrace me as a friend, I had no clue how to be a friend. In my youth, the children I went to school with that I thought were my friends also went to church with me. They treated me one way at church and then trashed me at school. Because of their behavior, I had no idea who to trust and I was always afraid that the same thing would happen again and again. I had to learn how to be healed before I could move forward.

From my experiences, I learned that it is important to walk in your own truth and not someone else's. Embrace who you are from your head to your toes. Here is an exercise to help you:

1. In the morning after your shower or bath, look at yourself in the mirror.
2. Thank God for every part of your body.
3. Tell yourself that you are uniquely created in His image.
4. Remind yourself that you are necessary for the Kingdom.
5. Create your own personal affirmation of who you are in Christ.

Healing belongs to us all, and you are entitled to be healed and whole to use your gifts and talents in fulfilling the purpose for which you were created. We all have a part to play in this earth. There is no one person who is not an integral part of the bigger picture. You are not an afterthought. You were created for a purpose. You are needed! We are all necessary; there is not one person who exists who was born by accident. Our Maker is the Giver of Life and He knew that each of us would be born. He knew us before we were in our mother's womb. Our arrival did not catch God by surprise. It is our responsibility to live our lives to please an audience of one: God. I keep thinking about when we'll stand before His throne and He asks us what we did with what we were given. We cannot blame Juju for why we did not fulfill our assignment. We are accountable for our own salvation.

I finally got tired of pretending. I got tired of smiling when I was not happy. I hated who I was because I really did not *know* who I was. I knew that the person I had become was not the person I wanted to be. I knew something had to change or I was going to end up in a rubber room! My journey to becoming the "real me" began when I gave God complete control of my life. No longer would I try to protect myself from others. I would allow the Holy Spirit to live through me and make me who He wanted me to be.

When I was hiding and pretending, I was not walking in my true purpose for the glory of God. When I would start to do something, I would actually participate in self-sabotage, because I did not think I deserved anything that was good. If enough people keep telling you that you are no good, you will eventually believe it...if you are not transformed by the truth of God's word. It is human nature to tend to believe the worst of ourselves.

You know how it is...we can receive ten compliments and one word of criticism. Now tell me, which statements would you most focus on? Nine times out of ten, you'll dwell on that one negative comment as opposed to relishing the ten compliments you received. Think about this: With as many people as there are in the world, why do you get so caught up in the minuscule percentage of those who do not have anything good to say about you? Why does it matter?

We accomplish our purpose by using the innate abilities given to us by the One who created us. If we want to know how something works, we don't ask the "creature," we ask the creator. We do not ask the car how it gets fixed. We take the car to the mechanic to get it repaired. We are to go to God and ask Him how we use those things we are passionate about for His glory.

You are a "Designer's Original." You will not find another person on this earth like you. You may find someone with whom you have common likes and dislikes, but there is only one you. Let's put it this way: If you robbed a bank and left a fingerprint behind, the authorities will look for the person that matches the fingerprint...YOU! No one else will be on their radar.

I encourage you to walk boldly in who God created you to be. I found that when I embraced who God created me to be, I met (and continue to meet) so many people who resonate with my story and the assignment given to me. I am on a mission to meet the needs of those assigned to me. I encourage you to do the same and I hope you shine!

As an international speaker and a transformational catalyst, Pastor Darlene Thorne, M.Div. has traveled extensively, speaking at conferences, and facilitating workshops and symposiums. With a focus on total self-care, she delivers a message of life change from the inside out! Featured on television, radio and live sessions, Pastor Darlene presents a clear, life-changing message that motivates others to live a life of pure authenticity. Married to Pastor Kevin Thorne, Sr. for over 30 years, they pastor Grace Worship Center in Clayton, North Carolina, and are the proud parents of two young adults.

FROM SHAME TO SHINE: A JOURNEY

Caroline D. Parker

"For God, who commanded the light to shine out of darkness, hath shined in our hearts . . ."

II Corinthians 4:6a

Perhaps it was because I was born on a Palm Sunday, but I've always had a strong, deeply spiritual bond to Almighty God from childhood. Another factor for that bond was the fact that Mama was a preacher's kid. She had a strong, unshakeable faith in God and was the most spiritual person I knew. Because of her profound spirituality, I have...at the core of myself...a deeply rooted sacred connection to God and His Kingdom. But I also grew up fearing God to the point of hating to read the Bible and sometimes feared God Himself. As the granddaughter of a fundamentalist Baptist preacher, my thought process skewed more toward fire and brimstone than deliverance and joy.

An only child for seven years, I was alternately doted on or chastised. Because of the mixed signals I received, I grew up feeling that I had to be perfect to get my needs met. I felt that, not only was I not "good enough" within the culture of my mother's educated, accomplished family, I believed that God didn't love me either. A family dictate to "not embarrass our good name" held me in an emotional straitjacket. I was desperately afraid to do the wrong thing, because I didn't want to get yelled at or punished. "Only children" have the spotlight placed squarely on them because there's no one else to deflect the attention. So, I grew up feeling that I had to be correct and on guard at all times.

The only thing I ever received positive recognition for was being "smart." I was a good student and loved school in the early days. Unfortunately, I was also a "quirky," overweight, "bookish" kid who wasn't in tune with my peers...and I got teased a lot. As tough as things were, they went seriously downhill when I got my period at the tender age of 8. My early menstruation caused my father to become even more protective of me because I was now a baby who could technically have a baby. After my early onset menses, life was never the same for me. I incorrectly internalized my period as being a "dirty" thing and developed a deeply rooted sense of sexual shame, especially as I grew up and boys came on my radar. The overprotective reaction of my dad anytime I was around a boy added to my feelings of confusion.

One day I took the trash out to the big rusted fire can in our backyard. Some boys were playing basketball in the alley and their ball bounced over our fence. I handed it back and stood watching them for a minute. They weren't remotely interested in me...but Daddy saw the exchange through the kitchen window and called me in. He accused me of enticing "those boys" and smacked me across the face. I was ten years old! Around the same time, I was taking an innocent walk around the block with my little sister Valerie who was almost three. When we came around the corner, I saw some boys from my elementary school riding their bikes. We chatted about how cute my sister was and other harmless stuff. As we talked, my dad came careening around the corner in his car. He spoke harshly to the boys and told me to get in. As soon as

I got myself and Valerie situated, he hit me across the head and accused me of trying to meet up with and flirt with "those boys." One of them saw him hit me, and he told all the kids in school that my father had popped me good. On top of all my shame, I now felt humiliated.

After that slap in the car, something changed in me. Because I read a lot from an early age, I was a pretty happy kid with a generally sunny outlook on life. But after all the punishment I got, I became hurt, angry and resentful toward my parents and my family. I felt there was nobody on either side of my family to help me deal with my feelings...nobody to help me process my turbulent flood of emotions. I began using food even more to stuff down every feeling I experienced, good and bad. Eating large quantities of food temporarily took away my pain and self-loathing. It also caused me to be grossly overweight all my life because I "ate" my feelings rather than deal with them.

When we don't deal in our truth, we develop patterns of behavior that keep us from honest connections with ourselves and the people around us. Because I was too scared to admit what I was really feeling, I developed a strong fear of being judged. I learned to walk into a room or event without really looking at the people there. I didn't want to make eye contact, because I believed everyone would look at me and judge me for my weight. After being regularly teased for my obesity, my "white way of talking" and my supposed "uppity-ness," the seed of anger grew and I was in an internal war between hope and despair. To compensate, whenever I felt people just didn't "get me," I developed an air of superiority so I wouldn't feel the pain of their taunts and jibes. I became relentless in my quest to be known for my "smarts." I had some successes in school, and from the outside, looked to be doing okay. But in truth, I refused to bear witness to my inner pain, or the self-loathing I felt the more I ate my feelings away. I would not admit that I was upset that my younger cousins were successfully navigating the "family mandate" to get a college education. They were graduating, whereas I dropped out of The University of Michigan-Dearborn after two years because I, the "smart one," felt too stupid and my pride would not let me ask for help.

Pride. Pride in a human is like tarnish on a golden object. We will never shine with the light of God as long as we are out of order and let pride take prominence in our soul. I think of Nebuchadnezzar and how God warned him what would befall him if he didn't change his prideful ways. In my overblown pride, I wished for my intelligence to get me out of the humdrum, unhappy life I was living. I knew that if I could just get the "right" job and meet the "right" people, I'd have the "right" kind of life I deserved. Yes, I said "deserved"...because that was my mindset after decades of stuffing down my truth. Pride led me to believe I was above it all and "deserved" to live a life that accommodated my smarts. However, God knew better and, like Nebuchadnezzar, He tried to warn me about the path I was on by trying to break through my emotional armor to show me He loved me as I was, perfect or not. He just wanted me to walk honestly before Him and trust that His love and Jesus' sacrifice covered me.

He sent the first warning about my behavior after I finally graduated from UM Ann Arbor. Armed with a bona fide bachelor's degree, I wore that achievement like Queen Elizabeth wears her crown. I was on my way! I was going to have the best job and the best life; and at last, I'd reap the rewards of my intellect! That was my fantasy. My reality was that I couldn't pay anyone to get me a job. Every door was shut to me from 1991 until 1995. During that period of time, I reluctantly went to Social Services to apply for Medicaid. I mean...*really*? Me? The UM graduate? When I stepped my educated self up to the counter to ask what I needed to do, the clerk tossed an application at me and brusquely told me to sit down, fill it out, and wait my turn. I got highly offended by her attitude. I looked around at everyone in the office and decided that I was better than this. I followed my righteous indignation to the parking lot and threw the application away. I felt a tremble in my spirit that my attitude was wrong, but I overrode it. After all, I was a UM graduate and Medicaid was for "poor people." (O, forgive me, Jesus; but yes, that was truly my mindset at the time.)

Other warnings came through a tsunami of trials. I suffered the death of my mother in 1995, which devastated me. This was followed by my father's and best friend's deaths in 1999. That same year, I had a breast cancer scare and was involved in a devastating split with family members. I sat in my house...sobbing...asking God why my life was such an unholy wreck. I'll never forget the answer I got that day in the soft stillness of my bedroom. I had a vision of miles of concrete with sharp, jagged colored pieces of glass glinting out of it as far as you could see...reds, blues, yellows, greens.

God told me: "This is your foundation from childhood. The jagged pieces are teachings and beliefs you absorbed and behavior you've shown that have kept you from truly knowing Me. But I will build a new foundation within you." As the enormity of what He said flooded me, I heard Him again: "This transformation will be painful, but I will guide you through."

Flash forward to July 2009. I was living in a room in the basement of yet another cousin's house. It had no windows, no light, no ventilation and no heat. I had moved over twenty times since Mama's death, staying with various friends and relatives. By then, I was just grateful to have a roof over my head. I overstayed my welcome at my cousin's home and she told me I had to move; she needed that room for her growing family. (Back then, I felt totally rejected, hurt, and scared; but now, I absolutely "get it" and will be forever grateful to her for her letting me stay there for as long as she did.) The only option I had—because I had run out of places to go—was a homeless shelter. Oh, how I struggled with that in the darkness of my little basement room. As Jesus did in the Garden of Gethsemane, I begged God to take this cup from me. I questioned Him. Why hadn't His promise of a new foundation and a new life come to pass yet? Where was He in this situation? Why had He let me get so low? Oh, I raged and was in such dark anguish. I felt so hopeless that I thought it would be better if I just died. Who cared anyway?

One day, I came up out of the basement after everyone had gone. The sun was glowing like melted butter on the walls of the living room. I felt like I had stepped into God's Shekinah Glory because the room shimmered with a golden radiance. For the first time in weeks, I felt God's love and peace.

I sat quietly before Him and spoke my truth: "Father, I don't like my life and I do not want to go to a homeless shelter."

Months of pent-up emotions overwhelmed me, and I bowed my head for several moments letting them flow over me before God.

"Nevertheless,"...I could barely speak..."You must have a lesson for me to learn, so I will humble myself and go. All I ask is that you mercifully let me learn the lesson as quick as possible so that I can be better."

As soon as I finished, something melted inside of me and I knew that God heard my cry. A few days later, my closest sister-cousin Sherri Sims called me. I told her what happened and asked her to pray for my strength to handle shelter life. She prayed mightily, and though I was still a bit nervous, I felt stronger. I was determined to see this test through and look for a shelter. A few days later, Sherri called me back and said: "Caroline, I just realized. My house in Jackson is available. Come down here. You don't have to pay me any rent...just take care of the utility bills if you don't mind."

I don't have words to express how the light of God flooded my spirit or the relief I felt. Because I had finally and truly reached "nevertheless," He graciously showed me He already had a ram in the bush waiting for an authentically humble response from me.

After I let go of that final shred of pride, God brought me to Jackson, Michigan. I moved into Sherri's house in July 2009 with the help of my very good friends, Mark and Maralyn. I moved, not knowing that I was going to experience God's promise of that new foundation through circumstances I could not imagine. I wrote in an earlier anthology, "It's Possible: Living Beyond Limitations," how God cured me in 2010 of multiple myeloma, an incurable and sometimes fatal bone marrow cancer. As of this writing in 2017, I have been declared free of multiple myeloma, and my oncologist is puzzled that I have absolutely no symptoms of that original "incurable" disease. I told him it was because of my faith in God's Word...particularly Luke 9:1-2.

With Sherri's help and blessing, I moved from her "shelter house" into a beautiful senior apartment complex in October 2010. It was here, in 2013, that I finally faced the last remnant of my childhood shame. I decided I would not despise the gift of life God had given me by healing me of two different cancer diagnoses. In every other area of my life, I had found a measure of success. But my obesity was still a giant millstone around my neck. I went to the University of Michigan's bariatric program and went through the process to have a gastric bypass. I was one session away from setting a surgical date when I received a second diagnosis of DCIS breast cancer. I was told I could not have bariatric surgery until I was cancer-free for one year. After a volcanic inner meltdown, I folded spiritually. I didn't talk to God or my family or do any activities for weeks because I was so grievously, bitterly disappointed.

My weight increased until I couldn't even walk well without a cane. At that moment, I knew I had to lose weight or I'd be permanently crippled...or die. But I had never before been able to lose weight the "natural" way.

Sick and tired of being sick and tired, I sat down in my meditation chair and faced the devil head on in blazing anger. I told him: "My weight has been my biggest stronghold because of you, my emotional overeating, and my past stinking thinking. It ends now!" It felt like Satan laughed at me and my old panic and fear rose up. At that moment, I wanted to eat something. I took deep, calming breaths and looked to the Lord. I told Him how scared I was to face Satan on my own. I told him I doubted I could lose weight without surgery, because the devil had always been too powerful in this area of my life. I told him I doubted my ability to overcome this burden and begged him to help me and show me the way. After that, I sat still until His peace came over me. I turned my TV on and the first thing I saw was an ad for Medical Weight Loss Clinic. My initial thought was "Yeah, right...as if there's one here in Jackson. It's probably in Lansing."

So, I went to KFC for dinner (I still laugh at the irony), a drive I regularly did. But this time, when I got to the corner to turn right, the Holy Spirit said, "Look up there." I looked, and a sign on a marquee I'd been driving by for years jumped out at me..."Medical Weight Loss Clinic." That was on a Tuesday. I came home and set up an appointment for that Thursday and I haven't looked back. I've lost over 100 pounds since July 2016. I still have 150+ pounds to lose and I still sometimes struggle, but I am determined that my faith in God will get me to my goal. At that point, I want to have skin removal surgery and fully live the life for which God created me.

I give God the glory for changing my relationship to eating. I eat to live now; I no longer live to eat...and I eat more mindfully. I also no longer beat myself up when I eat off my plan. I just make better choices the next time.

Since my weight loss, I ditched my quad cane and use only a single cane when I need to walk on uneven ground. I lead cardio drumming several times a month and was captain of my Wii Bowling team. I exercise on the NuStep 3 times each week and I want to buy a Schwinn bicycle to ride around my complex. Every day, I rise and praise God for another chance to do better. I thank Him for His blessings, grace, forgiveness, deliverance and mercy in bringing me through so much.

I am a living witness and a walking miracle as to the greatness, goodness, power, and faithfulness of Almighty God. If I could talk to you personally right now, I would say that you are alright just as you are. I promise that you can have a better life. You've read of my journey; and while you may have had different challenges, you can overcome them all through your faith. I encourage you to never let fear of feeling like you are "less than" keep you from seeking and especially trusting God for better in your life. I bear true witness that

God WANTS you to shine with His glory. He has ordained that you live the life He created you for, not the life created for you by others. Do not be afraid. I have faith you shall overcome no matter what you face. I have absolute confidence that God wants you to shine. And whenever things get difficult, please remember this: God and I ***believe*** in you...always.

Caroline D. Parker is an award-winning author, literacy advocate and budding drummer. She has a passion for God, sci-fi, literacy, the creative arts, cooking and travel. She earned a BGS from The University of Michigan and an MPA in Political Science (Health Administration) from Eastern Michigan University. She is committed to literacy and mentorship and helping women network with each other. She won first place in the Avery Hopwood summer award competition at The University of Michigan-Ann Arbor; was chosen first-place winner of a statewide writing contest sponsored by Presbyterian Villages of Michigan; and was published in an earlier anthology: "It's Possible: Living Beyond Limitations." She is a Resident Commissioner for the Jackson Housing Commission and a Board Trustee for the Villages of Spring Meadows in Jackson, Michigan. She also authors a blog: "Wisdom Woman: Thoughts Of A Quirky Mind" on blogger.com. Caroline can be contacted at cbane411@gmail.com.

OUTSIDE THE GATE

Minister LaVondia Eldridge

Who would have thought that an innocent trip to the store for snacks would turn out to be one of the darkest days of my life?

I left home on my way to school that day feeling good. I felt confident, happy, friendly, and carefree. (I was also looking very cute, I might add.)

I remember it was warm and sunny on that early summer day. We had a couple more weeks of school until summer break. Neither jacket nor sweater was needed. It was a perfect day...so perfect that the students played nice in the schoolyard. The yard of our elementary school was a great big open playground...a space where we were free to safely roam, run, laugh, and play. Everyone seemed to get along that day. I was determined not to fight that day; after all, I was not dressed for fighting. I was wearing my green skirt, a white ruffled blouse, and brand new white-wedged sandals. It was a small wedge of course; in fact, they probably didn't even qualify as a true wedge. But oh, how I had begged for those sandals, convincing my mom I was ready for them. I even had on panty hose; how's that for growing up? I liked the way I looked and felt that day. I was growing up and becoming a woman. Well, maybe not a woman, but definitely a young lady. I had dressed myself and I felt good about the choices I had made.

The neighborhood corner store was within walking distance, not at all far from the school. (How cool was that?) I had never left the yard to venture to the store before, though I had heard that many students had done so several times over. They bragged of their successful venture, made it sound adventurous, and they had the snacks to show for it.

Because I really wanted to know the process involved in going to the store, I asked lots of questions. Was this venture really as easy as they said it was? I was sure I was up for the challenge, but I needed just a little bit more convincing. So, one day I asked my slightly older cousin to confirm that it was easy to leave the school grounds and not be noticed. She said "yes," and admitted that she used to do it.

I'll never know for sure the exact moment when it locked in my mind that going for snacks was something I wanted to do. I believe it could have been right after speaking with my cousin that the seed to do it was planted. So, let me get this straight (I thought to myself): leaving the school grounds to make a quick run to the store was an easy task...a quick adventure...and all I had to do was simply walk outside the gate, go a few feet to the store and BAM! I'd return in enough time to go back inside the school (with my snacks) and no one would ever know.

Maybe because of how I felt that day, maybe because of the weather, or my new level of confidence (I don't even know), I decided that today would be the day. I determined that it was a "now or never" moment and I had the courage to do it. I was going to go for it, and even if I had to go alone; it did not matter.

And just like that, I did it. I stepped outside the gate. I left the school grounds. When I looked back, no one seemed to even notice. I was free!

I was walking fast, adrenaline pumping. I'm halfway there but now it's hotter than ever. The sun is pointing directly at me in all its glory. I'm sweating. It's taking much longer to get to this store than I had anticipated. Who thought of this? All of a sudden, I thought, "This is a dumb idea. Who does this, and why? And who said the store was only a short distance? It's miles away, or so it seems. I should not have done this!" "This will definitely be my last time doing this," I promised myself. Finally, I make it to the store and now I stand there confused. In all my inquiring, I never asked what snacks I should buy. I am literally the proverbial "kid in a candy store" and I don't know what to get because there are too many options. I made it all the way here and now my biggest hurdle is deciding what candy I want.

While in the store, I became extremely nervous. This is, after all, the neighborhood family store, and I'm pretty sure they know my family. What if they had my mom's number or the number of another family member? I'm trying to not make eye contact with the cashier, because I'm certain they've seen me in here before...though never by myself. Surely my being here is a red flag to them, I am thinking. To make matters worse, out of my peripheral vision, I see a man watching me. He is lingering a few aisles over in the back of the store. I become extremely uncomfortable. Clearly, I didn't think this through. I did not think anyone else would be at the store this time of day. I pay for my candy and rush to get out of there. I must get back to the school before anyone notices I am gone!

I get out of the store and take a deep breath. Wow, this is a lot to process! None of what happened was ever in any of the stories I'd heard about sneaking off the yard to get snacks. I must not have gotten the whole story or else I would have stayed inside the gate.

But for now, I did it. Whew! Cool! I made it! I have my candy and I'm heading back now. The school is only a block away, and because it is in view, it seems like going back is easier than leaving had been. Hey, that wasn't so bad. I'm so close to the yard that I can see the faces of some of my schoolmates. I have to just cross the street; then I'll be safely within reach of the gate.

Wait! Is someone behind me? I'd better pick up my pace. I make eye contact with my friend, Krystal, who knew of my plan. She's approaching the gate to meet me and I quicken my steps.

All of a sudden, just like that, I didn't make it back safely! I never get to Krystal! I never make it back inside the gate! It turns out that the man in the store...the man who had been lingering a few aisles over...had followed me. I remember now that I had seen him very briefly while walking to the store; but I had been so caught up in the experience of my journey that I was not consciously aware of my immediate surroundings. Suddenly...just as I was headed towards the gate...he grabbed me from behind, put his hand over my mouth, and dragged me across the street. He pulled me into the alley, threw me against a garage, and started to rip off my clothes. He yelled explicit instructions, but I did not move fast enough for him. In fact, I couldn't move at all! I was in shock. I could not comprehend what was happening to me. I was completely frozen; my senses were dulled. He was angry; and although I was numb, I felt the intensity of his anger with each blow to my face as he mercilessly beat me. Within seconds, my inner light was dimming until my candle felt completely blown out. As I felt myself fading, my only thought was: "Why did I ever step outside the gate?"

I was in a daze, but I vaguely remember a lady who appeared...seemingly out of nowhere! She must have been taking her trash to the alley; but to me, she was an angel sent by God to save me from further hurt.

I cannot tell you what happened after that, because I was no longer present mentally. I was in a dark space because of what happened to me. I thought that somehow this assault was my fault. I blamed myself for leaving the school grounds that day. I was embarrassed. I was deeply ashamed. I was humiliated. I no longer felt lively and carefree. Instead I felt limp and lifeless. I no longer felt like a young girl almost in her teens who had liked the way she looked and felt earlier that morning. Now, I felt like I had aged. I felt heavy, down, and dark. It felt like “lights out” for me. My very countenance had changed.

My story of leaving the schoolyard would never be like those of my classmates. Mine was not a tale of a successful venture and return, but one of a ferociously inhumane assault. I got more than I bargained for when I went to get my snacks. I was more than hurt...I was devastated and ravaged. My face was swollen; my eyes were puffy and black. The bruises beneath the surface were indescribable. I was now unrecognizable. I felt small. My trust was gone. My brutal attack ripped me to the core. Not only did I lose my pretty sandal in the struggle, I lost all my self-confidence. I lost my “happy” and retired my “friendly.”

I stopped wearing dresses, skirts and even pantyhose. No more wedged sandals. I did not want to be noticed. I felt I had lost my voice. I felt powerless.

God used my favorite teacher at that school to help walk me back into the light of existence. She told me she saw me as a beautiful little girl, inside and out. She told me that I was not alone...and that the same thing had happened to her as a young girl. She told me I had to get back up and keep moving. She said many things during the many conversations we shared. She was a safe place for me...away from the painful memory of what had taken place that day. She told me to take back my power and to be thankful that God intervened and stepped in at the exact moment that He did. She said that things could have been worse...that it was a blessing that I lived to tell my story. When she said that someday my story would help someone else, she gave me the courage to breathe. In the middle of my darkness, I felt an internal flicker of light and wanted to live again. Her words of encouragement were powerful, because she herself had to emerge from a darkness of her own. I knew she could relate. I was standing where she had stood many years prior. I knew that, if she could make it out of her dark place, I would also be able to shine again. She gave me hope when she shared her story; it opened me up and gave me strength to go on.

Many cases of assault, abuse, rape, molestations, and more go unreported. It is not your fault if you have been the victim of something horrible. You are not to blame for your stolen innocence...for sick minds or misguided appetites. No, you are not to blame! Tragic situations and circumstances in life sometimes will occur. Things may have happened to you where darkness tried to suck you in and choke the very life out of you. The darkness has not comprehended that you can shine even in the midst of the darkest dark. Your brilliance is not to be compared to that of mere man because the Holy Spirit dwells within you. Therefore, you shall shine brightly!

Let prayer and forgiveness help walk you back into the light of your existence. Do whatever it takes to emerge from the darkness. Join a support group. Get therapy. Seek counseling. Talk to someone. Don't hold in your truth. Break through the chains of darkness by using your voice. If you hold your truth within, it will eat at you like a cancer. If not dealt with, it will show up later down the road. Unresolved issues can typically show up at the most inopportune time in your life...well after you think you've handled them. Whatever has happened to you...whatever truth you hold...you may have pushed it down so deep into the crevices of your soul that you may have blocked them out altogether. But they are still there...lingering, waiting for a safe release. You may have been or felt like a victim, but now it's time to rise. Take your stand as the victorious woman that you are. Much prayer helped me. I had a praying grandmother who regularly sowed the seed of prayer. In fact, I was told later that, around the time of my assault, she was praying for me. I believe God heard her prayers and stepped in and intervened. As horrible and as dark as that day was for me, I am aware that things could have been worse.

Truth is the only thing that is solid. Truth pierces the darkness and shines a big, bold, bright light on the ugliness within the shadows. When the light comes, the darkness is no more. It's time for you to shine. It's time to walk in the glory of your shine. We tend to hide whatever we are in bondage to. The pseudo feelings of shame and guilt only desire to cripple you. Those negative feelings give way to passageways that lead to bondage and disparity within the darkness.

Truth to power is this: You are not what you have been through. Things have happened along your journey, and unfortunately you cannot detach yourself from those things. They did occur. But you are no longer outside the gate. You must pull up, reach up, and defy the unmitigated gall of "darkness." It has tried to hold you down for too long. The truth is, the darkness is afraid of your shine. When you step on the scene, the darkness must flee. And too often, you have not sent the darkness packing because you are too afraid to face and expose it.

But I offer you hope today. I light your candle with my truth. I declare unto you that, even in your darkest hour, you are beautiful. There is hope. The sun will surely shine again in your favor. You will make it. You will come out of whatever has happened to you. You will shine victoriously...bright like a diamond. But first, you must GET UP! Arise, and take back your power. Tell your story. Tell your truth. Light someone else's candle, and you will add to the strength of your own light by sharing your truth. Be encouraged. Believe that what you are dealing with now is temporary. It won't always be like it is right now. Your past moments of darkness...your present circumstances...they do not define you. You are beautiful and you are powerful. You are a force to be reckoned with. Your voice is needed in the land today, especially for those coming behind you. Someone is waiting to hear your voice, your story, your truth. It is the thing that will give them their freedom.

When you stand and open your mouth, you will shake off the dust, the dirt, and dark scars of your past. You will emerge from those dark places to take your rightful place in the light. And I say to you, may your every chain be broken.

Be empowered this day. Share your story. Not only will others experience freedom, but so will you, just as I have by sharing my story. And the brilliance of your shine will be like a magnet...drawing, pulling, and uniting other wounded women together on a level of common ground. Together, we will all shine! We will eradicate many forms of darkness and unlock many gates as we walk in truth...releasing the power and the radiance of our SHINE!

Minister LaVondia Eldridge is a licensed minister and ordained prophet who was born and raised in Detroit, Michigan. She has attended Detroit Public Schools, Bishop College of Dallas, Texas, Kingdom and Faith Bible College of Detroit, Michigan. She graduated from the School of the Prophetic Global Ministry in 2004. She has worked with youth and singles groups, and God uses her to minister to women. She is under the leadership of Apostle Joseph and Pastor Brenda Hobbs at Triumphant Life Christian Church in Highland Park, Michigan. LaVondia flows heavily in the prophetic, teaching and preaching the Good News of the Gospel of Jesus Christ. She has a heart for broken women, desiring to see them made whole. She speaks at women's retreats, conferences, and seminars. She preaches the Word of God with power, boldness, conviction, and a heart of compassion. She loves the Lord and desires to see change—not only in her own life, but also in the lives of those she is blessed to be able reach.

SHINE SPECIAL FEATURE: UNDERSTANDING THE NEW RULES OF MONEY

Jewel Tankard
International Business and Media Mogul
with Andrea L. Dudley
Visionary Publisher

I remember the moment well when I first came upon the phenomenon that is Jewel Tankard. In February 2017, I was scrolling through Facebook when I came upon a video entitled, "Women Winning Conference LIVE." I was somewhat familiar with the featured speaker due to her highly visible profile, but before that moment I hadn't followed her career closely. The sound quality of the video was bad, yet I felt compelled to continue listening to her because what she was saying deeply resonated with me. She had my attention. She was speaking about women, finances, legacy, and compound interest. Each of these words was music to my ears. The message coming from this woman was unique, different, intriguing, and mesmerizing. As I listened, my soul lit up and I knew that, whatever she was doing, I wanted in. Needless to say, soon after that fateful Facebook encounter, I achieved my goal of being "in," and Jewel Tankard became my business coach and mentor. Through her, I joined a company called iMarketslive, where I was privileged to learn about investing in Forex©, a foreign exchange currency market. I am officially an investor in this $5.3 trillion a day industry. Hands down, listening to Jewel Tankard's presentation and being blessed to work with her is the best business decision I've ever made.

The Kevin Costner movie, "Field Of Dreams," has a tagline which says: "If you build it, they will come." Costner's character was led to build a baseball diamond in his cornfield based solely on a nameless voice that spoke life to his dream. In my own life, I also had a dream of financial freedom that I had seriously prayed about for some time. I wanted to learn how to invest money and funds wisely. But in all honesty, as time passed, I wondered if I had missed out on opportunities to learn more about investing. Though I didn't see how I could find an opportunity to make my dream come true, I resolved in my heart to never give up hope.

For years, my dream slumbered in the deep recesses of my soul, and life went on. From time to time, I thought about investing, but I didn't seem to be led toward achieving my goal. I remembered a prophetic word spoken to me in 2005 by Apostle Jane Hamon.

Apostle Hamon told me: "'I will give you supernatural keys for prosperity; not just for individuals, homes, and families but for entire communities,' says the Spirit of God."

Wow! What a tremendous word! I was up for the challenge, but through the course of years gone by, I hadn't come across the vehicle whereby this prophecy would manifest in my life. I have always known that I was called to empower others and help them reach their destinies; and in many ways, I was successful. When I watched that presentation on Facebook LIVE, Jewel Tankard's words were the key that finally unlocked the closed door to my dreams and answered my prayers.

With any assignment given by God, divine connections are made with people who have the ability to equip you and help you fulfill your assignment. For instance, Deborah needed Jael to help finish her assignment. Without Naomi, there would have been no Ruth. And without a Lois, there would have been no Eunice. Partnerships are very powerful. I am tremendously blessed to be in partnership with Jewel Tankard. In her, God has given me a complete package, because she is a master mentor, trainer, and coach. Please allow me this opportunity to introduce Jewel to you.

Jewel is an economist by profession and a graduate of the University of Michigan. She is a native of Detroit who was blessed to be born into an entrepreneurial family. She is the star and matriarch of Bravo's hit reality series, "Thicker Than Water." The wife of Gospel jazz musician Ben Tankard, she is also a pastor and business mogul who desires to see women and families live their dreams. Jewel is a multi talented woman of deep complexities. She is a mom, a sister-friend, a talk show host, a business and entertainment mogul, and a savvy real estate investor who likes to have fun and live life on the wild side. She firmly believes that "You Can Have It All!"

Jewel traces her interest in financial independence back to her early days in Detroit, Michigan, aka, the Motor City. She fondly remembers how her parents owned the first African-American record shop in downtown Detroit.

Jewel relates, "Growing up, everybody would come into the store whenever new records would be released by such great vocalists as Minnie Ripperton, The Temptations, Phyllis Hyman, and the Whispers, to name a few. I grew up in that environment and saw that [her parents] had a very strong work-ethic. Seeing them work together and do it so well was inspirational. They also reaped the benefits of their success. They had his and hers Rolls Royce's, his and hers Mercedes, and I had a Volvo. Seeing all of that and being exposed to housekeepers, cooks, and drivers was a lifestyle I became accustomed to early on in life."

Unfortunately, the good times didn't last forever; the family suffered through trying times and Jewel herself endured many unpleasant bumps in the road.

"In the 1990's, we lost everything," she shared. "When that happened, I was devastated. I wanted to recreate the lifestyle my dad had created for us, so I started dating drug dealers. After a couple of years, they started getting indicted or dying, and so I went to church. I remember telling God: "Lord, I'm giving my life to you."

She laughs: "Honest to God, one of the men in my life was a drug kingpin, and I thought I could pray him out of that lifestyle!"

Though her life didn't change overnight, it began to transform the more she experienced God's Word.

"After about six months, I realized that [the drug world] wasn't in God's plan for my life. I also realized that, instead of looking for a daddy, a boyfriend or husband to create the dream of how I wanted to live, I needed to create my own economy. This decision made me change my major to economics," she states.

In coaching calls with Jewel, who is a master coach, we are encouraged in our personal development, provided with quality mentoring, and challenged to change our lives by dreaming big and being open to new ideas. She inspires and encourages us to develop our financial "gut" and listen to our instincts.

Jewel also strongly believes that prayer and fasting is essential to success. She is committed to giving people, especially women, a picture of what is possible. She candidly shares the principles she used to make the transition from working for others to owning her own successful business. In doing so, she helps others who want the same kind of financial freedom to live the life of their dreams.

Through her unique business message, which is built upon a strong Biblical foundation, Jewel helps ordinary women lead extraordinary professional and personal lives. She leads by example by maintaining a positive and hopeful outlook on life that helps motivate others to reach their fullest potential. Her positive outlook and faith is at the core of the Jewel Tankard Brand and sets the tone for her television talk show and her wildly popular series of financial workshops, "Millionairess."

For the past year, Jewel has traveled across the country expounding on "the Cashflow Quadrant," and "The New Rules of Money" as written about in Robert Kiyosaki's book, Rich Dad's CASHFLOW Quadrant: Rich Dad's Guide to Financial Freedom.

She is unwavering in her advice to women who want to be financially free.

"Just start, that is key," she states firmly. "You need to make a decision that you will start and learn something new, because the new rules of money look nothing like the old rules of money."

She continues: "The old rules of money were to get a job, have a traditional 401(k) and sit with an adviser from Edward Jones once a year so they can tell you to invest in an annuity, CD, and/or mutual fund. Unfortunately, all of those products only bring in 4-8% interest per year and inflation is 11% interest per year. This is why no one is getting wealthy off their 401(k)'s, and also why baby boomers have to return to work; they are not making enough money to retire on, especially because they are living longer."

She further says: "Another new rule of money is to start trading in foreign currency—you can produce cash flow every day and only need a minimal investment to begin making good money. You can start by buying gold or silver bullion, in fact, an ounce of silver is only $20."

She also encourages women who want to be investors to start a group or club to better assist one another.

"The 'Millionairess Club' is so important, because most people do not trust their financial gut," she relates. "Everyone has a financial gut, so when I see a deal, before I know anything about the deal, I can sense if this is something that I need to do or not. The club is for women who are used to asking their husband's or boyfriend's permission for things that they shouldn't have to ask permission for. If I have an instinct in my gut that I need to buy this apartment building, then I need to trust that, because maybe my husband doesn't have the capacity to counsel me on it. Most of the time the answer will be "no," just because he may not understand what I am trying to do. So, I have to be careful that I don't allow somebody else's lack of understanding keep me from trusting my gut."

"A lot of women lose the fight in the process," she acknowledges. "At the end of the day, you may want to put a demand on your husband to make it happen for you, but you need to think about what you are going to do for yourself independently. You can control what you do."

"Trusting my gut is ultimately what's going to bring me to my wealthy place" she explains.

I am very blessed to have Jewel Tankard in my life. Through her, my financial knowledge has expanded and she has truly helped me to become more financially astute and independent.

Dr. Jewel Tankard is a financial expert through hard-earned experience and is also the star and matriarch of Bravo's hit reality series "Thicker Than Water." The wife of Gospel jazz musician Ben Tankard, Jewel is a pastor and business mogul who desires to see women and families live their dreams by obtaining financial freedom. She is also a Forex Investor who is helping to change the financial trajectory of families throughout the world. To learn more about Jewel Tankard and the Millionairess Club, please visit her website at www.jeweltankard.com.

Excerpts attributed to:

http://www.blackenterprise.com/money/bravos-jewel-tankard-new-rules-money/

SHINE LIKE A DIAMOND? CAN I GET OUT FROM UNDER THE DIRT FIRST?

Evangelist Valerie Parker Robinson

> *"Diamond, shine bright like a diamond, shine bright like a diamond,*
> *shining bright like a diamond...We're beautiful like diamonds in the sky."*

In 2012, Rihanna's song "Diamond" reached the top of the music charts. Her song won the Top R & B award in 2013 at the Billboard Music Awards. In 1949, Carol Channing sang a song entitled "Diamonds Are A Girl's Best Friend" in the Broadway play, "Gentlemen Prefer Blondes," which was later immortalized by Marilyn Monroe after she sang it in the 1953 film adaptation of the play. (I'll share a Carol Channing tidbit later.)

Who doesn't want to shine like a diamond? Who would scoff at being a girl's best friend? While you may be hard-pressed to find someone who doesn't like to shine brightly or wear the best gem that God created, you will find that many people want the shine and the glamour of the diamond life, but don't want to go through the actual process that creates that shine and brilliance. In fact, I believe if you surveyed the women within your sphere of influence, you may hear them say, "Yes, I want to shine like a diamond, but can I get out from under the dirt first?"

According to the American Museum of Natural History's website, most natural diamonds are formed at high temperatures and pressure at depths of 87-140 miles inside the earth. Diamonds can be formed in the earth's interior but not near the surface. Diamonds are also formed in the bottom of the seabed at depths of 125 miles beneath the sea floor. The only reason diamonds are ever found near the earth's surface is because great heat has pushed them up from deep within the earth's core. Can you imagine the heat and pressure it takes for a diamond to get to the surface of the earth? Can you imagine yourself going through the stress and trauma that it takes for a diamond to be mined? And what about the work that must take place to get that diamond ready for a merchant to sell? If we are truthful, many of us have had to be forced out of the dirt called "Our Life" in order to become the women we are today.

Dear Reader: May I share one of my "dirt" stories with you? My dirt experience was painful, it was humbling, it hurt, and it shook my self-esteem to my very core. I felt betrayed, weary, and worn out. And yet, in all honesty, it was also one of the best learning experiences I could have ever gone through. Why? Because I learned, while in the dirt, that there are others down there who also experienced or were experiencing the same emotions and feelings I was going through. Some had been underground in their dirt experiences for a long time; and some were just entering their experiences and wanted to shine, but they did not know how to navigate their way back to the surface.

In 2011, I had just turned forty and decided to go back to school and get my Master's Degree in Business, majoring in

Organizational Management. Back then, I was not as computer literate as I am now. In fact, the last college paper I had written during my undergrad years was done on a typewriter! I was also old enough to be the mother of 90% of my grad school classmates. To show you how behind the eight ball I was...when I had to do my first team paper, I missed my deadline because I retyped all my team's papers into my own! I didn't know anything about copying and pasting words from other papers into one document. Yikes! Beloved, I am telling you that when my teammates showed me how to copy and paste, I felt like the heavens had opened up, the angels were singing, and God had given me a gift straight from His Throne Room. The members on my team hated putting our papers together, but I gladly volunteered to do them now that I had this new "copy and paste" tool in my arsenal!

After graduation, I was offered a position in my company that was the perfect job for me. It was my dream job, as a matter of fact. However, I had to turn it down because it meant traveling five days a week, coming home on Friday, and flying out again on Sunday evening. I had a daughter who was just starting kindergarten and I didn't want to leave her, so I declined the position.

At the time, I was told by my manager that, if I didn't take the position, I would never be asked to take another one. I told her I couldn't take it. Even after a few days of being asked to reconsider, I stood my ground and told her I wouldn't be taking the job. Little did I know that saying "no" would be a decision that would cost me in furthering my career. But back then, my decision was one that I knew was best for my child and for my peace of mind.

The years went by and so did positions. It turned out that I was never approached to take another job within my company. But God's hand was with me, and He prospered me and allowed me to do what I needed to do for my family. He taught me how to grow financially and invest the monies I made wisely. I met friends and gained influence among my peers, and God protected me every time there were rough periods in the company.

In December 2014, I decided to apply for one of three managerial jobs that opened up within my department. I had the credentials, the education, and the backing of my fellow officemates. I decided to throw my hat in the ring and interview for a position. If I got the job, I would be managing a team that was doing a job I used to have many years ago...and one I was still sometimes called to do whenever a major catastrophe happened within the United States. I felt equipped with an inordinate amount of knowledge, people skills, and empathy, to lead the team to a greater level. My colleagues were very supportive once the news traveled that I was interviewing. I felt there was a genuine joy and excitement shown towards me leading up to my interview date. I was confident in my ability to interview and present myself well. I was ready.

I called my sister-friend Pamela Taylor before my interview began. She had me take a selfie so she could make sure I was dressed appropriately and to her liking for my interview. (Gotta thank God for sister-friends who have your back!) I sent it over to her and she approved. She also gave me words of encouragement. On the day of my interview, coworkers came by my desk to wish me good tidings and in I went. Afterward, I felt the interview went well; I had been prepared and was feeling upbeat.

I was out on vacation for the remaining two weeks of December and was told to expect a call from the recruiter with the outcome of my interview. I was on vacation when I received a call from the recruiter that I had NOT been chosen for the position. My mind went on autopilot, but I heard him say it was not my credentials that were lacking, it was just that management decided on three other candidates. He said a manager would be available to speak with me if I had any other questions. To say I was devastated was an understatement. I was in Myrtle Beach with my family when I told them what happened. They were sad for me and were in disbelief as well. As I walked along the beach, I couldn't help feeling like the earth was shifting, sending me deeper into its core. I was descending into a dark place.

Not getting that managerial position was the beginning of my underground experience. I felt darkness overtake me. I felt the dirt of failure. The ghost of my decision years before to not take that position haunted me. My world imploded. I was embarrassed, angry, bewildered, and hurt. I didn't even call my coworkers because I was trying to wrap my head around being rejected. The enemy pounced with every thought of self-doubt and deception he could throw at me. Of course, why wouldn't he take advantage of my deep feelings of hurt? Doesn't he always come when you are at your most vulnerable? The sting of rejection was so very strong and powerful, especially as the news of my not being chosen circulated throughout the office.

The names of the employees who got the positions were announced. Even though I was on vacation, my phone was blowing up with calls from friends and coworkers who couldn't believe I hadn't been chosen. So many people called who had been rooting for me to get the position and who just knew, beyond a shadow of a doubt, that I had it in the bag. With every call and every text, more dirt kept falling on me. I was sinking deeper and deeper into the underground. I was so hurt that I could hardly pray.

All I could muster was, "Lord, You know what is going on. Lord. I am hurting, but I am trusting You."

Some days, I would lie in bed and sigh: "Lord, I can't see my way out, but I trust You."

Then there were days when the weight of the earth felt unbearably heavy and all I could do was just think the words, "I trust you, Lord."

I went back to work. It would be wonderful if I could tell you that the darkness had lifted and the cherubim and seraphim were heralding my return with song, but that would be a great big lie. The truth of the matter is that I became like Zechariah: I stopped talking. I couldn't bring myself to talk to anyone at work except my trusted sister-friends. I wasn't the bouncy, bubbly self that I normally was. For once, I didn't try to lift the spirits of those around me. To be honest, they were on their own. I stopped talking for two months. I went in, did my work, and went home. I was afraid of what would come out of my mouth if I talked, so I never did. Going "dark" did not make people feel comfortable and, to be honest, I didn't care if people were not comfortable with my silence. Withholding my light felt good. I spoke when I was spoken to but other than that, I had nothing for nobody. I was underground, and it felt good that the ones on top of the earth were uncomfortable. I did my work and handled my customers, but other than that, everyone else was on their own until...

"Val, can I talk to you for a moment?"

I heard a small voice call out to me as I was walking down a hallway. I went towards the voice and a coworker pulled me into a side room.

She told me: "You are so calm...even though you didn't get the position. You aren't even hollering or acting like it bothers you at all. You are so at peace."

Huh? What? I was looking at her talking to me and was thinking to myself: "What is she seeing that I am not seeing?"

I stood there, bewildered by the words that were coming out of her mouth. She went on to tell me, with tears in her eyes, that she had been applying for other jobs for years and had never been picked either. She said she was on the verge of giving up; but she had been watching how I was handling my situation, and she had been encouraged by my peacefulness.

After I regained my composure, I was able to minister to her by telling her how I was really feeling. I was transparent about my hurt and my anger; and she was blown away when I told her the real reason I had been silent. She had thought it was because I was so strong, but I told her it was my weakness being made perfect in the strength of the Lord. She wasn't the only one who pulled me into corners and conference rooms to tell me of their struggles on the job. There were many...too many to count. They were the walking wounded.

Hurting people had been suffering all around me; but I never knew of their struggles until I was in a place where I could feel their infirmity. There were others who were being cultivated in the underground dirt of life whom I would have never met if I hadn't gone through my very public trial. As I shared my story, I was able to help lift those whom God sent to me to the top of the earth's crust again. As I was pushed up,

I was used to push others up. The scales of my eyes were falling off to all the hurt around me. I felt that God had given me the great honor of seeing the hurt of His people as He saw them.

It was after that initial conversation, and other moments afterward, that I felt myself being thrust up towards the surface of life again. The dirt that had been covering me had actually been working for me, forcing me to leave all my insecurities and my feelings of inadequacy down in the underground. When its work was done, I emerged from God's protective cocoon back into the "Son" shine.

I learned how powerful my voice was, because when it was hushed, it had a rippling effect upon those who were in my sphere of influence. I learned that I am an atmosphere changer. I learned that there is a lesson in every painful experience we go through. I learned that, in every loss we think is bad, God will change it to our good.

My story ends well. After this experience, I was given the opportunity to co-chair a resource group for women in my company, which allowed me to travel, meet new people, and pour into their lives. I was tasked with onboarding new hires into our company by helping them navigate their new corporate surroundings. In December 2016, God let me know that it was time to retire. He told me it was time to shine in a new sphere of influence...photography. Just as a diamond or a prism reflects the light, God has blessed me to capture all the reflected glory of His magnificent creation through the lens of my camera.

Side note: Remember how I wrote earlier about Carol Channing and Marilyn Monroe? Most people don't remember that Carol was the original singer of "Diamonds Are A Girl's Best Friend." Most remember Marilyn singing it. That struck me, because it recently came out that Carol Channing was African-American, but she passed as white because she thought being black would stifle her career. She was in her eighties when she acknowledged her heritage. She was a woman who felt she couldn't live as she was born to be. What a tragic way to live. God created us to shine brightly.

We are accepted in the Beloved! So, let's SHINE!

Evangelist Valerie Parker Robinson accepted the Lord as her personal savior at the age of eighteen and has served in multiple ministerial capacities. Valerie is married to Melvin G. Robinson and they have one daughter, Chelsea Glenn Robinson. Valerie attends United Christian Fellowship in Wayne, Michigan, under the leadership of Senior Pastor Shane Pringle and Lady Deena Pringle. Valerie is an ordained minister and chaplain who has ministered in various venues in the United States and Canada. Valerie is a two-time contributor in the internationally released, "Talitha Cumi" book series with her stories entitled, "Have Faith in God" and "Cancer Is Not A Death Sentence: A Sister's Perspective." She is also a highly sought after, acclaimed professional photographer of corporate events, family photos, nature and wildlife pictures, and domestic animals.

CONCLUSION

Andrea L. Dudley

Earlier in this anthology we talked about the need to discover your authentic self. Once you have found your authentic you, you do not ever want to lose you again. However, maintaining your authenticity may be challenging. The pressures of life can weigh you down or try to make you "fit in" with the status quo. Being authentic takes work, determination, and a defined purpose or a true understanding of who you are in the universe. It is easy to morph into something or someone you were not created to be.

> ***Maintaining your authenticity is of absolute necessity if you are going to shine.***

9 Steps to Live True to Yourself

Step #1: Do You

I encourage you to journey to the very center of yourself. Stop making apologies for who God created you to be. There is a phrase that says, "Get In Where You Fit In." I would like to coin another phrase: "Get In If You Fit In." There are certain situations that will compromise your authenticity if you make yourself "fit in." Finding where you fit in allows you to be you. If you do not fit in, do not beat yourself up about it. Keep looking. Your "tribe" is looking for you. They are seeking you just as much as you are seeking them.

I attended a seminar in Detroit hosted by Bishop Corletta Vaughn. The special guest was First Lady Myesha Chaney, wife a preacher from Los Angeles. She was on a book signing tour for "Hiding Behind the Lipstick" and was also the guest speaker. At the end of the presentation, she offered each woman an opportunity to write the things that have held her back or hindered her. It was called their "lipstick" confession. She then invited those women who were brave enough to share their lipstick confessions with the group. Several women shared and vowed to stop hiding behind their lipstick and live in their authenticity and purpose.

Be brave and true to who you are. Stop wearing unnecessary masks just to fit in or avoid facing the reality of who you are. Those masks can make life feel hopeless and imprisoning! Even in a crowd of faces, it is easy to feel lonely if you are not being yourself and if the people around you do not appreciate who you really are.

Refuse to give up your seat of authenticity.

Come to the front of the bus. When you are your authentic self, you not only invite others to be authentic, you become a bright watchtower for the people you wish would find you.

Step #2: Step into the Wilderness

My husband Michael and I lived in Adrian, Michigan, for several years. I call those my wilderness years...my Egypt experience. During wilderness experiences, you find out who you really are and what you are really made of. Your destiny is often revealed and magnified in your time in the wilderness. In the wilderness, you become vulnerable, naked, and humble; and you are forced to face your fears. The enemy of your destiny lives in the wilderness waiting to pounce on you. He offers you a life of grandeur if you will just comprise who you are. He wants you to bow down, serve, and follow him. Mediocrity lives in the wilderness as do lack, drought, and fear. Your enemy encourages you to deny your destiny while in your wilderness. The wilderness is dry and hot, and dehydration is imminent if you do not find water. The tempter lives in the wilderness and says he will give you anything you want if you will only forget this nonsense of doing what you were created to do. In the midst of his attempts to throw you off your game, you can find peace if you will stay within your authenticity. Remember, the tempter is a fraud.

A fraud cannot offer you authenticity.

"The clearest way into the Universe is through a forest wilderness." —John Muir

Step #3 – Infinite Intelligence Is Speaking. Are you listening?
Your life's purpose has already been discovered. Listen closely to the conversation that is going on inside of you. The more you pay attention to this conversation, the more you will want to listen. It takes practice to hear this guidance, just as it takes practice to hear your heart's desire, to trust your gut, and to listen to your intuition. Infinite Intelligence leaves clues. These clues are what will lead you along destiny's path. You have the ability to live a life that is true to who you are...a life that you really want. Listen like your life depends on it.

"Creativity comes from trust. Trust your instincts." — Rita Mae Brown

Step #4: Count the Cost and Do It
Make choices that put you above everything and everyone else...even those you love and cherish the most. If you do not take care of yourself...if you do not do what is best for you, your relationships will eventually suffer. Trust in the fact that

doing what is best for you *is* best for everyone, even if it does not feel like it at first. Sometimes sacrifices have to be made. People will get hurt and there will be losses, but the rewards gained from following your heart are absolutely everything in comparison. Do something difficult, for no other reason than you like to do it.

> ***"Every day we have plenty of opportunities to get angry, stressed or offended. But what you're doing when you indulge these negative emotions is giving something outside yourself power over your happiness. You can choose to not let little things upset you."***
>
> ***– Joel Osteen***

Step #5: Believe

Whatever you think, that **is** your truth. Let me paraphrase what Henry Ford has said:

"If you think you can, you are probably right. If you think you cannot, you are probably right." Believing in yourself is essential to your living authentically. Many people fail because they give up before they even try. Do not stop believing in yourself even for one second. You have to push beyond your unbelief, your doubt, and your fear. Unbelief cannot hide. It is out in full view. When you believe in yourself, you exude a certain aura. You attract success. Even if your towel is sweaty or filled with tears, do not throw it away. Persevere! Keep believing...no matter what.

> ***"Some people say I have attitude—maybe I do, but I think you have to. You have to believe in yourself when no one else does—that makes you a winner right there."***
>
> ***– Venus Williams***

Step #6: I Am Not My Hair

In America, a great deal of value is placed on our outer appearance, especially if you are an African-American woman. It is very important to get clear on the fact that you are more...so much more than how you look. India Arie penned a song titled, "I Am Not My Hair."

Here are some of the lyrics of that song:

> Does the way I wear my hair make me a better person?
> Does the way I wear my hair make me a better friend?
> Does the way I wear my hair determine my integrity?
> I am expressing my creativity...
>
> Breast Cancer and Chemotherapy
> Took away her crown and glory
> She promised God if she was to survive
> She would enjoy every day of her life
> On national television
> Her diamond eyes are sparkling
> Bald headed like a full moon shining
> Singing out to the whole wide world like, HEY!

You see, it has never been about how you look...your shape, your color, your race, or even your hair. You are not your hair. It is about the light that illuminates from within. Let your light shine so that others will be drawn to that light and worship the Giver of that light.

Michael and I traveled the United States on a bus in a singing group called Festival of Praise. Every Sunday, we performed two concerts in two different churches in two cities that lay in close proximity to each other. After the evening performance, we would all wait excitedly to see who we would be paired with for the night. We all hoped to be selected to go to some luxurious home for the night with an aristocratic looking family with two children, an able-bodied mom and dad with a dog and a cat. (Well, let's leave the dog and cat out since I am allergic to both.)

One particular Sunday evening they said, "Michael and Andrea, you are going home with the assistant pastor and his wife." To our dismay (and because of our small mindedness), he was about four-foot-nine and a paraplegic. He could not even help us with our luggage. He and his wife lived on the campus of the church, so we did not have very far to go. We were glad for that.

That night, staying in their modest abode was a life-changing experience for us...so much so that the residue of his impact on our lives lingers on even today. That man ministered to us so very profoundly that we vowed to never, ever judge a person by how they looked ever again. We were ashamed and convicted of how we pre-judged this giant of a man. He was living his truth in his authenticity and it changed our lives. On Monday morning, we awakened, received our bag lunch, and began our travels all over again...and were grateful for the opportunity to have met this precious soul. The light that illuminated from him burned so brightly that his being a paraplegic was a non-factor.

Do not allow how you look to limit what you do. Allow your light to shine brightly and live out your truth.

"Beauty is not in the face; beauty is a light in the heart." — Khalil Gibran

Step #7: You Are the Master of Your Own Fate

Everyone is born into a family. Sometimes, the environment in which we are raised places limits and boundaries upon us which must be broken. Break free! Do not allow the limitations of your parents or family members hold you back. You have the power within to do whatever you set your mind to do. Use your foundation as a springboard to thrust you forward.

You are the architect of your existence.

"Every great dream begins with a dreamer. Always remember, you have within you the strength, the patience, and the passion to reach for the stars to change the world."

– Harriet Tubman

Step #8: Become Whole—Nothing Broken, Nothing Missing

You must learn to love you—flaws and all. The healing salve of love will heal your soul, your body, and your spirit. Every experience, good and bad, creates the fabric of your life. Your experiences shape you. When you accept that you are where you are in life because of the decisions that you have made, you give yourself permission to change. Hurts, disappointments, and pain no longer paint the canvas of your life when you live in your authenticity. The Creator of the universe loves you with an everlasting love. When you accept this love, you open yourself up to live and to give love in return.

Wholeness awaits you. Open and receive.

"A man cannot be comfortable without his own approval." – Mark Twain

Step #9: Enter Into God's Rest

Sometimes I have trouble resting. Sometimes my mind is racing with thoughts and ideas that are filled with emotions. I have to purposefully and intentionally bring my thoughts to quietness.

A rested mind can tap into your authenticity.

Living authentically means living in the purpose for which you were created. It means trusting that your Creator has your back. One of the definitions of the word "relax" is "to become less firm." Thus, relaxing your grip on your own life, career, family, etc., and giving them over to God in faith is the best way to relax. Your mind may be bombarding you with a list of all the things that you need to do, but simply ignore it and rest. Erase your agenda. Clear your mind. Rest.

So God blessed the seventh day and made it holy,
because on it God rested from all his work
that he had done in creation. (Genesis 2:3)

ACKNOWLEDGMENTS

My mother was a bright shining light who didn't say much; but when Vera spoke, everyone listened. It is because of her strength, faith, and tenacity that I have been able to overcome tough and challenging situations. Mom wasn't one to engage in drama and foolishness, but she was fun and reassuring. I get that from her. I dedicate this book to her.

No matter what I do, I always have his support. He is always there to encourage me to go after my dreams. He is always there to ignite my fire. He is my best friend and husband, Michael Thomas Dudley. Thank you for your ever-increasing patience, your love, and your commitment. I love you.

Without the assistance of Caroline D. Parker, I would have been hard pressed to finish this book. Her keen, unique, and stellar editing style makes this book a wonderful read, with consistent and endearing tones of light and love. Her sincere desire and passion to bring this anthology to life and print was inspiring. Thank you, Caroline, for the countless hours that you spent (with me and on your own), reading and re-reading the manuscripts to make this book amazing.

Linda Weatherly, from the very beginning...since 2007...when I didn't have a clue what I was doing, you helped me. As an editor, proofreader, and formatter, your keen eye and commitment to excellence made each author's story truly come to life. Words cannot express my heartfelt appreciation for you and all that you've contributed to these books. Thank you for taking this journey with me. You are a true friend.

Finally, thank you Solomon, my youngest son, and Valerie Parker Robinson for making each author look great at our photo shoot. The photos are beautiful. Rashida Williams, CEO of the Glam Studio and the Glam Squad did a fabulous job glamming us up at the photo shoot.

ABOUT ANDREA L. DUDLEY

Visionary Publisher, Speaker, and Transformation Coach

Andrea serves the world as a catalyst for change. Whether she is helping a client birth their book or speaking at a women's conference in South Africa, helping people discover their God-given life purpose is what gives Andrea great joy. Her love for people and her holistic faith-based approach embodies a message of empowerment, inspiration, and spirituality that helps others succeed in accomplishing their goals.

As the CEO of Habakkuk Publishing, Andrea has helped over 150 people become first-time, published authors through the acclaimed "Talitha Cumi" anthologies. Her signature writing and publishing program, "Birth Your Book In 90 Days," teaches writers how to self-publish.

As a Forex investor, Andrea is helping individuals, families, and communities increase their financial portfolio. The Forex, also known as foreign exchange, FX or currency trading, is a decentralized global market where all the world's currencies trade. The Forex market is the largest, most liquid market in the world, with an average daily trading volume exceeding $5.3 trillion. All the world's combined stock markets don't even come close to this.

As a speaker, Andrea has been featured in many conferences around the world: the BEST Conference, the SOAR women's conference, the Queens conference and W.I.L conference. Andrea's keen spiritual sensitivity enables her to zero in on the unique needs of her audience. Women are thrust into their destinies, and Andrea was thrust into her role as a spiritual leader and ordained pastor.

A dedicated and passionate scholar, Andrea received her Master of Science Degree and her Bachelor of Arts Degree from Western Michigan University.

Andrea has shared 35 happy years of marriage with Michael Dudley. She is the mother of Andrea, Solomon and Princeton, and the grandmother of Ashlyn.

Andrea is available upon invitation to speak at your event and can be reached as follows:

andrealdudley@yahoo.com or www.andreadudley.com

734.772.2079

OTHER ANTHOLOGIES IN THE "TALITHA CUMI" BOOK SERIES

Made in the USA
Columbia, SC
26 August 2017